Broadway, Balanchine, and Beyond

UNIVERSITY PRESS OF FLORIDA

Florida A&M University, Tallahassee
Florida Atlantic University, Boca Raton
Florida Gulf Coast University, Ft. Myers
Florida International University, Miami
Florida State University, Tallahassee
New College of Florida, Sarasota
University of Central Florida, Orlando
University of Florida, Gainesville
University of North Florida, Jacksonville
University of South Florida, Tampa
University of West Florida, Pensacola

UNIVERSITY PRESS OF FLORIDA

Gainesville

Tallahassee

Tampa

Boca Raton

Pensacola

Orlando

Miami

Jacksonville

Ft. Myers

Sarasota

Broadway, Balanchine & Beyond

A MEMOIR

Bettijane Sills with Elizabeth McPherson

Foreword by Carol K. Walker

All photos are from Bettijane Sills's personal collection unless otherwise indicated.

This book may be available in an electronic edition.

24 23 22 21 20 19   6 5 4 3 2 1

Library of Congress Control Number: 2018953483
ISBN 978-0-8130-5625-8

The University Press of Florida is the scholarly publishing agency for the State University System of Florida, comprising Florida A&M University, Florida Atlantic University, Florida Gulf Coast University, Florida International University, Florida State University, New College of Florida, University of Central Florida, University of Florida, University of North Florida, University of South Florida, and University of West Florida.

University Press of Florida
2046 NE Waldo Road
Suite 2100
Gainesville, FL 32609
http://upress.ufl.edu

To my late husband Howard S. Garson,

my son, Ben David Rosenthal, and

my dear friend Lucille Werlinich

Contents

Foreword

I have known Bettijane Sills for more than thirty years, as a colleague and as a personal friend. Through these many years, what has always been crystal clear to me is the respect and admiration she had and continues to have for George Balanchine. I distinctly remember one day in the Purchase College Conservatory of Dance when Bettijane came into my office very soon after I became Dean of Dance. She was both distraught and laughing at herself a little bit. "Carol," she said, "I know I shouldn't be upset, but today I realized that my students consider Mr. Balanchine to be history. To me he still is such a vital part of our world." I commiserated. The man had only recently passed away, but to our students in their world, yes, he was already history. To Bettijane, he was and continues to be a vital presence in her teaching and choreography and remains a monumental influence on her life. In this book, with love, objectivity, awe, and some humor, Bettijane shares details and reflections on her work with Balanchine and New York City Ballet during the historic "golden years" of the 1960s, as well as on her working childhood as a professional actor in New York City, her personal life in and out of the dance world, and her teaching career.

Bettijane Sills has given us a wonderful view into the world of a New York City child who began working in professional theater at the age of seven through her mother's influence, ambitions, and direction. She enjoyed her acting career, her evolving stage names, her lessons, and, to enable her burgeoning career, the Professional Children's School. Her musician father was a large influence on her, while her relationship with her powerful mother, who lived to be 104, was conflicted. However, through her mother's ideas and attention to her theatrical education and career, Bettijane found her real love, classical ballet. She studied at Balanchine's School of American Ballet, and through her talent and devotion actually achieved the dream of so very many young girls: she was invited to join New York City Ballet. What a wonderful, exciting life. Bettijane takes us on her journey through being a student to joining the company; to being cast in ballets; to being in the studio where Balanchine, the master, created work on her; to touring the Soviet Union on a State Department–sponsored trip during the Cold War; to her battles with weight; to suddenly finding her name removed from the rehearsal/casting lists; and finally, to her decision to leave the company. She writes about the exquisite feelings she had while dancing *Serenade* and *Concerto Barocco* and how and when she learned many other ballets by Balanchine as well as by Jerome Robbins, John Taras, and Jacques d'Amboise. What an incredible place she earned in the world of classical dance to be in this amazing company for eleven years, on stage night after night, performing some of the greatest ballets ever created in the history of dance.

The balance of her book is a journey of relationships, marriage, and career changes, circling back to Balanchine and ballet as she transitions to being a teacher, répétiteur, and choreographer. Her work in the Purchase College Conservatory of Dance, staging Balanchine's ballets, has given hundreds of students incredible and life-changing opportunities. Perhaps over the years, Bettijane's stagings of Balanchine ballets have become almost too much taken for granted as "normal" repertory events for us. We were the first college to be granted permission to perform Balanchine ballets, and we have performed more than any other college dance program. The incredible privilege for students to perform his work was so rare, especially in the 1980s and early '90s, that there was a bit of reverence about it all. Bettijane was originally entrusted by Balanchine himself (through Barbara Horgan) to pass on his choreography to these exceptionally lucky, young, preprofessional student dancers. When Balanchine passed away, the George Balanchine Trust became the keeper of the flame, having the final say about staging the works. They always, always, approved Bettijane's requests. And we, the Purchase Dance Company, were given permission to tour Balanchine's works abroad to Macau and twice to Hong Kong. This opened windows into the worldwide use of his work in professional training programs. Bettijane's love of the work shines through when staging the ballets. Through her coaching, the dancers truly convey the Balanchine "style," covering space with devotion, energy, speed, musicality, and grace. And how the students grow artistically through these rehearsals and performances!

Bettijane Sills has had an enviable life in the dance world. She takes us through it all.

Carol K. Walker
Founder and director, Global Dance LLC
Dean emerita, Purchase College School of the Arts

Introduction

Many years ago, I asked the late Francis Mason, noted dance critic and historian, if he had any thoughts about me writing my memoir. He discouraged me, saying that I needed a "hook," which seemed to imply that my life wasn't interesting enough to attract readers. After all, I hadn't slept with Balanchine; I hadn't taken drugs; I was just too "normal." So I did not write at that time. Then a few years ago, my late husband Dr. Howard Garson and good friends Dr. Peter Liebert and his wife, Mary Ann, began encouraging me to write about my life, and I once again began to consider my memoir. In beginning to write and piece the chapters together, I came to realize that although I may not have the specific "hook" that Francis Mason thought was necessary, my life and career provide a clear lens for understanding George Balanchine's choreographic practice, as well as the immensity of his influence on his dancers specifically and the dance field more broadly, simply because my career was not clouded by scandal or serious trauma. My performance career did not result in great fame or fortune, but nonetheless it was meaningful on many levels. My life postperformance career traversed through the joys and tribulations of teaching, choreographing, and staging Balanchine works. Although my life and career have had many turns and twists, I have worked in the dance and theater fields for almost seven decades.

I was an actor on Broadway and on television throughout my childhood, and, as one might guess, a parent, in this case my mother, was the driving force behind my career. My first Broadway role was at the age of seven, and I continued acting until high school.

While I was acting professionally as a child, I was also studying at George Balanchine's School of American Ballet. The skills I developed through acting allowed me to enter New York City Ballet at age nineteen, with prior knowledge and understanding of performance etiquette, energy, and how to connect to an audience. I was given roles such as Frau Stahlbaum in *The Nutcracker*, the Duchess in *Don Quixote*, and The Wife in *The Concert* (by Jerome Robbins) that allowed me to use my acting skills. These roles, of course, were in addition to the many roles I performed in the huge and vast range of the New York City Ballet repertory.

Balanchine (or Mr. B, as we called him) was a great teacher, and working with him in classes and rehearsals was life-changing. Performing his choreography was a whole other level of artistic education. His ballets are beautiful to appreciate from the observing side, but dancing them is an almost indescribable kind of joy. And *everyone dances* in his choreography, from principals down to corps de ballet, unlike older ballets in which the corps de ballet often acts as a kind of ornament. Although I probably didn't think of it this way when I was in the company, looking back I realize that I was part of an incredibly important artistic movement led by the greatest choreographer of the twentieth century.

My stories overlap with the life stories of many actors, dancers, and choreographers. The connections are endless. This book tells their stories as they intertwine with mine. For instance, I watched the rise and fall of Suzanne Farrell during my years with the company. Suzanne was sixteen when she joined New York City Ballet, just a few months after I did. Balanchine loved the way she moved, and so he made beautiful ballets for her and fell in love with her. When she married another man, he was truly devastated, and that devastation affected us all. Balanchine's affairs with his dancers, who, in several cases, became his wives, can be looked at adversely. I wish to dispel some misperceptions that might exist among students and nondancers concerning his attitude about women.

However, my greatest trial during my years with NYCB was not related to Balanchine's love life but rather to my own inability to maintain my best performance weight. Mr. B was a very patient man. Just as he waited for his dancers to perfect a step that gave them trouble at first, he waited for me to lose weight, which I did, numerous times. He would give me roles, and then I would gain back the weight, and he would take them away. It became a vicious cycle until finally he ran out of patience, which I understood completely. I was musical and loved to dance, and he recognized that, and so I was rewarded on talent and hard work—but only when I also kept the extra pounds off. I realized ultimately that I was conflicted, that part of me wanted to reach my full potential as a ballet dancer, to be successful, *really* successful as a Balanchine dancer, and part of me wanted to get married and have a child. In my world at that time, the two were not compatible. Mr. B would say, "Have affairs, dear, but don't get married." And having children was clearly discouraged. In his own quiet way, he demanded complete allegiance. As he ran out of patience with me, and I ran out of steam as a dancer, I got married, left the company, and had a child.

Through it all: love, marriage, divorce, and death, through career setbacks and incredible opportunities and accomplishments, I have moved through life as a Balanchine dancer. Working for Balanchine, working with an artist of that magnitude through my teens and twenties, shaped me not only as a dancer but as a person, and certainly much later as a teacher. He was a father figure to me, my artistic father. I was the obedient daughter, who wanted approval from the powerful daddy, who always did what she was told and never demanded anything from him. But he gave so much to me. Mr. B chose me as a dancer to enact his visions during the height of his choreographic career, and he molded my understanding of ballet and, even more broadly, artistic expression and how to be a performing artist—the responsibilities and the commitment required.

As a teacher, I am passing on his legacy, and it is through teaching that I have had my largest impact. Hundreds of students have passed through my classes in the Conservatory of Dance at Purchase College over my more than thirty years there, and I have conveyed Balanchine's legacy with the utmost care. So many teachers contributed to my artistic development, but Balanchine was foremost. I strive to convey his style and technique through my classes and through staging his work. It is through dancing his choreography that I believe students begin truly to understand who he was as a choreographer, as a genius. "Doing" is entirely different from watching or reading about a ballet.

I sent Mr. B an invitation to my wedding in 1971, while I was still performing. In response, he sent me a case of red wine, Nuits-Saint-Georges, and a note that simply said, "Remember me." As if I could ever forget him.

Chapter 1

Child Actor

Me as a baby, 1943. Photo by Morris Siegel, my father.

I was born on October 31, 1942, to parents Michael Morris Siegel and Ruth Siegel. In my early childhood, my mother was a stay-at-home mom. Professionally, my father played the double bass throughout my childhood. He was in the Pittsburgh Symphony Orchestra and St. Louis Symphony Orchestra when I was quite young. We moved back to New York City for my father to join the Radio City Music Hall Orchestra. My mother was a New Yorker, and my father, although born in what we know as Poland today, considered himself a New Yorker as well. I think they had been looking for a way to get back to the city. We lived on 107th Street, on the Upper West Side of Manhattan. It was a one-bedroom apartment, and my parents gave me the bedroom and slept on a foldout couch in the living room.

My dad performed regularly with the Radio City Music Hall Orchestra for what seemed like a long time. There were five shows a day, and ticket prices were reasonable. The shows were designed to appeal to everybody. The theater itself was opulent and grand, and the live production was breathtaking for me as a child. Shows would start with music from the largest theater organ in the world—the Wurlitzer—followed by the orchestra's overture. In addition to the live orchestra, there were the Rockettes, a ballet troupe, a Glee Club, and a "first run" movie, including cartoons and a newsreel. Sometimes, we would go to the 10:00 a.m. show at Radio City; my father would get us in for free when he was playing. The pit with the orchestra would rise as the movie ended, and my dad would wave to me as he came into view. It was so thrilling! During the years that my father was with the orchestra, Erno Rapee was the musical director from 1932 to 1945, and Charles Previn held the job from 1945 to 1947.[1] Alexander Smallens was hired as the musical director and conductor for the orchestra in 1947 and immediately began making drastic changes. The *Billboard* of September 13, 1947, reported that Smallens did not renew sixteen musicians' contracts and made the rest of the thirty-four members of the orchestra reaudition for him.[2] He brought in musicians he knew from other orchestras to fill the now open positions.[3] He also instituted a new rule that Radio City Music Hall Orchestra musicians could no longer hold other jobs.[4] This was a major shake-up to the orchestra.

Morris Siegel, my father, Riverside Park, circa 1945. Photographer unknown.

My dad was one of the musicians whose contract was not renewed, and it was very difficult for him. He had a nervous breakdown (one of three that I can recall) during which he became horribly depressed, needed to be hospitalized, and had electroshock treatments. It was a terrible time.

My dad was extremely talented musically and could also build anything and fix anything, but he had an enormous fear of auditions. In addition to playing the double bass, he was self-taught on the violin, and he had a beautiful bass baritone voice. He sang in twenty-five Broadway shows in the 1920s and '30s, among them *The Student Prince* (1924), *Princess Flavia* (1925), and *The Desert Song* (1926). He sang with Alfred Drake, who originated the role of Curly in the Broadway production of *Oklahoma!*. By the time I remember, however, my dad would only sing at home, sometimes in the bathroom and sometimes just in front of my mother and me. He had phobias that I never fully understood, and my mother became very frustrated by his fear of auditioning because it held him back from really being successful and making money. He had so much talent, but so little self-confidence.

I have always thought that my mother married my father because he was extremely handsome and in show business. My mom loved all his

Ruth Siegel, my mother, circa 1945. Photographer unknown.

talents. He was a great photographer, and he was a wonderful musician. She respected him for that, but she probably had so many bigger dreams for my father than he did for himself. After he lost his position in the Radio City Music Hall Orchestra, he mostly found work with touring productions, which was somewhat sporadic income. I remember specifically that he played with the Boston Pops. In looking back, I see that as my father's career faltered or at least became less predictable, my mother became more and more a driving force in my childhood acting career. I had an affinity for performing, but I am sure I would not have done all I did as a child without my mother's involvement. My mother was truly stagestruck and loved everything about the theater. She took me to see *Peter Pan* with Jean Arthur on Broadway in 1950 (with music by Leonard Bernstein), and soon I began to love the theater, too. I used to dance around the living room whenever there was dancing on television. I especially remember *The Ed Sullivan Show*, which ran from 1948 to 1971. It was hugely popular and always included featured performers like ballet dancers, actors, classical singers, pop singers, circus acts, and more.

When it came time for school, my mother enrolled me in the Riverside Church Weekday School for kindergarten. My mom and I were very close. I always cried when she left me, or so she said, but then I was fine once she was gone. I think probably my mother did not want me to attend public school in Manhattan, at least in the district where we lived, so she enrolled me in the Professional Children's School (PCS) for first grade. It was, and is, a school for children in show business, although I was not yet in show business. I think my mom had plans to put me on the stage, and that was another reason for sending me there. Perhaps she was envisioning an additional source of income but also just wanted me to be a part of that world so that she could be, too.

At that time, PCS was located on Broadway and West 61st Street, occupying three floors of a seventeen-story commercial building, not where it is currently but close. Because many students were working, with rehearsals, matinees, and evening performances, the school day was short, running from 10:00 a.m. to 2:15 p.m. If we missed classes, we were required to make up the work. When we were on tour, we kept up

My mother (Ruth Siegel) and me, circa 1947. Photo by Morris Siegel, my father.

with correspondence work. Even though there was a lot of flexibility, the expectations for academics were rigorous.

Sometimes after school was out, I would go with a friend of my mother's and her son to Chock Full o'Nuts in Columbus Circle (at 59th

Street) for a snack. I don't think I drank coffee then, but I know they had the best—heavenly! I would have their date nut bread with cream cheese or their cream pie and a glass of milk. They only had a counter, no tables, but the food was delicious.

As I began to be cast as an actor, being at PCS was perfect for what I was doing because it enabled me to complete my school work even when we were out of town doing Broadway tryouts in Boston, New Haven, or Philadelphia. I would work in the theater during rehearsal breaks, and I would send my homework back to school. The teachers would read it, correct it, and send it back to me. You had to be motivated, but I was, really compulsively so. I wasn't one of these kids who would just let schoolwork slide. My mother accompanied me when I had to travel, but she never had to push me to complete my schoolwork. However, so great was my mother's fear that if I missed a rehearsal I might lose my job that she sometimes took me to rehearsal with a fever and nasty symptoms when it probably would have been better for me to have stayed home in bed.

My classmates included actor Christopher Walken (who went by Ronnie then) and Jenny Hecht, who was the daughter of the great Hollywood and Broadway writer Ben Hecht. I was very good friends with Jenny and had sleepovers with her at her Nyack house and at the Hotel des Artistes. Zina Bethune was also a friend. In addition to being students at PCS, we also studied together at the School of American Ballet. Zina was a successful actor on screen and on television as a child and, as she got older, had a featured role on the TV series *The Nurses*. Her mother, Ivy, gave me acting lessons. Ivy was an actor and appeared in bit parts in movies. She would give me monologues that I would memorize, and then she would coach me on my delivery. My childhood boyfriend at PCS was Rex Thompson, who played Louis in the original cast of the Broadway production and also the movie *The King and I*. We even had a "mock marriage" ceremony. When *Peter Pan* came to Broadway, in 1954, with Mary Martin in the title role, all the children in the show were at PCS. Mary's daughter Heller Halliday became a close friend, and I went to Norwalk, Connecticut, to spend the night in their lovely home. The house was decorated beautifully,

Rex Thompson and me, circa 1950. Photo by Bill Staton.

and I felt proud that I was Heller's friend. I also got to go backstage and meet the great Mary Martin.

My time with my cousin Barbara Ley Toffler (whom I was very close to) and my other friends was the "normal" part of my childhood, and for that I am grateful. I was a working child actor and model, which very much influenced my childhood and the rest of my life. I loved my theatrical training and performing, but that part of my life was professionally oriented. I guess you could say that I had to be more of an adult than a child. With Barbara and my other friends, I could be a child and experience everyday childhood things. Maybe that is what allowed me to come out happy and well adjusted, as they say. So many

My cousin Barbara and me (*on left*), circa 1945. Photo by Morris Siegel, my father.

people who have been child performers struggle to manage their adult lives successfully.

As I moved into elementary school, my mother increasingly became a real stage mom—not quite a Gypsy Rose Lee stage mom but enough that she pushed me and really guided my career. My mother used to say to me later that I could have said "No" to a life on the stage, but I never felt I had the choice. There is actually a photograph of me (with Johnny Olson, the television announcer) in an article of 1952 called "Children Seen on TV Work Long, Hard Years" in the *Democrat and Chronicle* newspaper of Rochester, New York. Interestingly and insightfully, the article talks about how directors want children who bring their parents to an audition and not the other way around.[5] Who was leading whom was a bit ambiguous in my situation.

I had my first professional acting job in 1950 in the Broadway play *The Wisteria Trees*, which ran at the Martin Beck Theatre from March 29, 1950, to September 16, 1950. I was paid $50 a week, which I received on Saturday nights. The play was written and directed by Joshua Logan and was based on Anton Chekhov's *The Cherry Orchard*. It was produced by Logan and Leland Hayward and starred Helen Hayes. There were three children in the show, and one of the original little girls was underage according to union rules: She was six, which was too young to be working in a Broadway show in those days. Someone told my mother that they were looking for a little girl to replace that six-year-old. I was seven, so she took me to the audition. I got the part, which consisted of sitting in a chair and having Helen Hayes sing "Froggy Went a Courtin'" to me, and that was the beginning of my professional acting career. It was very exciting because I knew who she was and admired her greatly. I was billed as Betty Jane Siegel (which is my birth name). My mother changed my name throughout my career. She was always trying to find the least Jewish-sounding name. Later on it was Seagle, then Single and finally Sills. Betty Jane eventually became Bettijane.

My mother regularly bought the theatrical newspaper *Show Business*, and I was attending many auditions for plays and television. She would often lie about my age, saying I was younger than I really was, and she dressed me in very short little dresses.

Milton Berle (one of the producers of *Seventeen*) and me, 1951. Photographer unknown.

In 1951, along came an audition for the Broadway musical *Seventeen*. There was a part for a young girl, and it was for a featured role. I was very nervous at the audition, and I didn't do well and was not called back. I can remember the line I messed up to this day. I had to say, "He's barking like a big dog," and I mispronounced the word "dog" and said "dorg." My mother just felt I was meant to play that role, and my father asked the producers to give me a second chance, which they did, and I got the part. I was eight years old.

Seventeen ran from June 21, 1951, to November 24, 1951, on Broadway at the Broadhurst Theatre. It was produced by Milton Berle, Sammy Lambert, and Bernie Foyer. The music was by Walter Kent; lyrics were by Kim Gannon; and the book, by Sally Benson, was based on the novel by Booth Tarkington. I played the part of Jane Baxter, and I was billed as Betty Jane Seagle. Kenneth Nelson was in the play, too, playing my brother, Willie Baxter, a leading role. (He was later in the film *The Boys in the Band*.) The lead female was Ann Crowley, and Frank Albertson also had a leading part as Mr. Baxter. I see Frank Albertson in movies all the time now, the old black-and-white ones that run on TCM (Turner Classic Movies). It's fun and kind of odd to see this person I had worked with so many years ago. And there were two dogs in the play: an adorable, fluffy white Maltese named Perk, who played Floppit, and another dog, named Cookie, perhaps a mixed breed, who was very well trained and played Clem.

We had a "tryout" in Philadelphia first, and I discovered the Horn & Hardart Automat! They were the original kind of fast-food restaurants in the United States, and the first one opened in Philadelphia, in 1902.[6] They served cold food from little windows with doors that filled a whole wall. You could see what you wanted (like pies, puddings, cakes, and sandwiches) before you inserted your nickel or nickels and opened the little door to get the food. Hot food was served buffet-style. I was never a good eater as a child. My poor mother was always beside herself with anxiety over my lack of gastronomic intake, plus I was sickly, always coming down with tonsillitis or some other illness. I even had a case of mononucleosis, or what was then called glandular fever, when I was around seven years old and really was quite sick with that. Needless to say, I hardly ate anything. But in Philly, the Automat changed everything. I literally learned to eat there. I remember the cavernous main room with the lady behind the glass partition in the middle of that room. You would give her a dollar bill, and she would throw down ex-

Maurice Ellis and me in *Seventeen*, 1951. Photographer: Graphic House, Inc.

actly 20 nickels. (Everything was paid for with nickels). It was amazing how adept she was at throwing just the correct amount of nickels onto the marble slab. My favorite hot dishes were Salisbury steak and spaghetti with a red sauce. The most exciting part, though, was putting your nickels into the slot and pop! the window would open and there would be a slice of pumpkin pie or tapioca pudding. Sometimes you might even catch a glimpse of a worker's hand replacing an item once it was removed from behind the window. I continued to eat at Automats, but those first experiences have always stayed with me as vivid memories.

After Philadelphia we then had a tryout in Boston before opening on Broadway, and I had a very nice mention in *Variety*: "[T]here are only three guaranteed laughs, each delivered by juve actress Betty Jane Seagle, and all based on the stock gag of a moppet cracking wise in adult fashion."[7]

When we officially opened in New York, Brooks Atkinson, of the *New York Times*, described the casting and acting as "delightful all the way through" and specifically called attention to me: "little Betty Jane Seagle as Willie's scornful baby sister."[8] Arthur Pollock of *The Daily Compass* wrote: "The most satisfying member of the cast is a child named Betty Jane Seagle, who plays Jane, the Baxter brat, a self-possessed, forceful little actress with perfect timing."[9] In the *Daily News*, John Chapman wrote: "Little Betty Jane Seagle is captivating as sister Jane, and two of the best actors in the layout are dogs which are not identified in the program."[10] Walter Winchell, of the *New York Daily Mirror*, wrote: "[A]nd Betty Jane Seagle, a moppet who can mop up a robust laugh."[11] Finally, Marie Torre, of the *New York World-Telegram and Sun*, noted: "As Willie's sister, a tyke who sees all and knows all, Betty Jane Seagle is a little gem. But keep the little imp away from our house!"[12]

My salary was $75 per week in town and $100 on tour, which was substantial for that time, but it was certainly about more than the money for me. Being in this show was the most fun I had ever had, and I never got tired of performing the same part night after night. I loved it. The costumes, designed by David Ffolkes, were fantastic. I specifically remember wearing the most wonderful pink hat in the wedding scene. I turned nine while the show was running, so they had a birthday party for me with the cast, which was thrilling. After closing on Broadway, the show toured to Philadelphia. (We were supposed to go on to Chicago, but that did not happen.)

From this job, I started to get parts on television—*Studio One*, *The Philco Television Playhouse*, *Kids and Company*, *The Goldbergs*, *The Kathi Norris Show*, *A Date with Judy*, *The Paul Winchell Show*, and the soap operas *The First Hundred Years* and *The Egg and I*. I sang on *The Children's Hour*, a Sunday morning television show. It was sponsored by Horn & Hardart, the Automat owners. The show aired on NBC Radio in New York City in the 1940s and 1950s. It was really a showcase for young people with talent. The participants were not paid, at least not in my time, but I guess the thinking was that it could lead to other paid work. Rosemary Clooney, Frankie Avalon, and Bernadette Peters were some of the notables who got their start on the show. I also performed in a March of Dimes benefit and a Polio benefit concert. I learned a Japanese dance for a performance by the Children's Repertory Group. I did extensive modeling for publications like *Harper's Bazaar*, *Good Housekeeping*, and *Today's Woman*.

I remember being an extra in a movie filmed in 1954 called *It Should Happen to You*, starring Judy Holliday, Jack Lemmon, and Peter Lawford, which I recently saw on Turner Classic Movies. There on the screen were shots of the old Columbus Circle, and I saw the Chock Full o'Nuts and Childs Restaurant where my parents took me for pancakes with maple syrup. Such a treat in those days! So many memories came flooding back. It made me nostalgic to see those old shots of parts of New York, which are long gone.

In 1955, I was cast in a small part in the Broadway musical *Seventh Heaven*, which ran from May 26, 1955, to July 2, 1955, on Broadway, at the ANTA Playhouse. It was based on the 1922 straight play of the same name by Austin Strong. In this production, the music was by Victor Young; lyrics were by Stella Unger; the book was by Victor Wolfson and Unger; and choreography was by Peter Gennaro, with uncredited show doctoring by Jerome Robbins. There was lots of dancing in the show, some beautiful and stunning dances, but not for my particular part, which was small. The production was not all that well received. For instance, Lewis Funke, of the *New York Times,* stated: "Undoubtedly 'Seventh Heaven' has a proper place in the hearts of an older generation. But this edition is too much of a melange to retain the old mood."[13] I still enjoyed being in it. I was paid $100 per week.

Some of the cast members who were already or later became quite famous were Bea Arthur, Gloria DeHaven, Ricardo Montalban, Chita Rivera, and Lea (Becker) Theodore. When Chita Rivera did her one-woman show on Broadway not too long ago, I went backstage and asked her if she remembered me. I think she was just trying to be nice when

Seventh Heaven cast, 1955. I am to the left side of the photo with my mouth wide open. Photo by Will Rapport.

she said, "Yes, of course." But I remember her! A very dynamic dancer and performer. Bea Arthur was an interesting and surprising lady. Once, she was standing in the wings near the light board while they were calling the cues—cue 4, if I remember correctly. She reversed it to say "4 cue," which sounded like something else, if you can imagine. Ricardo Montalban was a kind man and always very nice to me. Barclay Hodges was another child in the show, and we kind of had a little romance going. I even invited him to my apartment on 107th Street. We shut the door to my bedroom, and I'm sure my mother was not happy about that. I don't think we were doing anything really R-rated. At twelve or thirteen, I was very inexperienced with boys.

In addition to acting on Broadway, I also saw a lot of shows. By the age of twelve, my cousin Barbara and I were traveling around the city by ourselves, and we would spend all day Saturday together. We went to see every hit show on Broadway in the 1950s when we were in junior high and high school: *My Fair Lady, The Most Happy Fella, Candide, Brigadoon, The Remarkable Mr. Pennypacker, No Time for Sergeants, South Pacific, The Pajama Game.* It was the Golden Age of Broadway, and you could get tickets for $2 or $2.50, nothing like the outrageous ticket prices today. Everybody went to the theater. Barbara and I would have lunch together (on our own) before the matinee performances at places like the House of Chan, Ruby Foo's (the original), or Tokyo Sukiyaki, which were in the theater district.

I performed in all sorts of other theater productions in addition to those on Broadway. One of these was in an Equity Library Theater production of a revival of *Annie Get Your Gun*, in 1957, which played at the DeWitt Clinton Adult Center in the Bronx and the Bryant High School Adult Center in Queens. I played Jessie, Annie's sister, billed as Betty Jane Single. It was directed by Jay Lee, with choreography by Matt Mattox and, of course, used the original music and lyrics by Irving Berlin.

The last play I was involved with was a summer stock production of *Meet Me in St. Louis*, in August 1960 (when I was seventeen), at the Sacandaga Summer Theatre, in Sacandaga Park, New York. We then took the production to Toronto, Ontario. Roddy McDowall and Joey Heatherton played the leads.[14] Hedda Hopper wrote that Roddy was per-

Annie Get Your Gun, 1957. I am on the far right. Photographer: Ottomar Studio.

forming in *Meet Me in St. Louis* to strengthen his voice for his upcoming role in the Broadway production of *Camelot*, which premiered that fall.[15] Roddy was such a hoot and told the greatest stories. We would go for lunch between rehearsals, and he would regale the whole cast because he knew everybody in Hollywood, including stars like Elizabeth Taylor and Judy Garland. He really was amusing.

The years between ages seven and thirteen were my busiest and most successful period in theater-show business. One part seemed to lead to another, and I believe I was making good money. The fact is that I never saw a dime of that money, as my mother used it for expenses—rent, clothing, food, school tuition, dance and acting classes, and so on. I can understand her reasons. We were not rich. My father was often away on tour and would send home a check for $100 periodically, and my mother was

Meet Me in St. Louis, 1960. I am fourth in from the left. Photo by Milton Tatar.

not working, at least early on, but I was. It was brought to my attention later on that a bank account should have been set up in my name and that the money I earned should have belonged to me. But it is long gone now. My mother did work some during my later childhood as a caseworker for the Department of Welfare. She would visit people in their apartments to determine if they qualified for welfare payments. She would go into low-income housing, always dressed well and in high heels. I would worry about her, but no one ever bothered her. Later on, she was given a better position in personnel, a desk job, which she really enjoyed.

Somehow, even with working, my mother managed my career in terms of taking me to classes and auditions. But perhaps more significant, at least on a psychological level, was my mother's handling of my career in terms of being supportive, or, in fact, sometimes not supportive. Once you do some work in the theater of any kind, you start to get more jobs, and so that was nice. My mother was proud of me when I would get a part, but I didn't always, and the rejection was painful for both of us. It was particularly difficult because my mother would get angry. She claims that she wasn't angry *at* me, that she was just angry that I hadn't gotten the job or that the little girl who had gotten the part was not as talented as I was. I disagree. I thought then and still think that she was angry *at* me because I disappointed her on some level. It was unfortunate that she could not control her anger in that regard. It was stressful; her anger was hurtful. But when I was chosen for a part, I forgot about the negative.

One of the worst incidents of her disappointment in me happened on my birthday when I was about nine or ten years old. I was scheduled to sing on the Sunday morning television show *The Children's Hour*, and later in the day there was to be a birthday party for me. I was really looking forward to that party. The program was live, as most television was in those days. There were some kids who were regulars on the show and then some who were on sporadically. My cousin Barbara had spent the night, and then that morning we headed down to the TV studio. I started my song and got through the first verse, and then as I started the second verse, I just blanked and could not remember the words. I somehow got it back together by the last chorus and finished it up.

My mother and my cousin Barbara were in the family viewing booth, and all I could think of was my shame at having forgotten my song. I knew my mother would be so embarrassed in front of all the other mothers. Even though I was able to pick up the lyrics at some point and finish, sure enough, my mother was furious with me. She wouldn't let up on me as we took the subway home, and then she continued on the street, walking from the subway. She was screaming at me that I had embarrassed her, and my cousin tried to intervene, but my mother was impossible. She just wouldn't stop. It was relentless. I wanted to crawl into a hole somewhere and disappear. She was a good mother on many levels, but that's one of those memories that has stayed with me for a long time and stayed with my cousin because she was very affected by it. My mother just made me feel that I had done a terrible thing, and most of all, that I had let her down. Looking back now, I can see my blanking out in a larger perspective—first of all, I was a child, and it was my birth-day; second, mistakes happen in live performance with performers of all ages; that is part of the thrill and the excitement. As my mother, she should have been talking me through my own embarrassment instead of screaming at me for embarrassing her. I think I carried the burden of these high expectations from my mother and my fear of failing her throughout my acting and dance career.

My relationship with my father was more distant because he was often away on tour, leaving my mother to raise me. But our relationship was also gentler. He was always kind and loving to me, although not always to my mother, which definitely made me feel uncomfortable. However, both of my parents were very overprotective and did everything for me, so much so that I was not learning to take on normal responsibilities that other children were at the same age. It is probably safe to say that they infantilized me some, partly because of my being an only child. My father even called me "the child." There is an often-told story that while cooking for a party that my cousin Barbara and I were giving for the New York City Ballet company when I was around twenty-one, Barbara handed me a knife to cut some tomatoes, and my father quickly took it away and said to Barbara, "How could you give the child a knife? She'll cut herself." My cousin responded, "She's twenty-one. If she has never cut a tomato before, it is time for her to learn!" As another example, my father washed my hair for years. Of course, this was in a New York City apartment, so he would rig up this platform where I would sit and then put my head on a board at the sink, and he would wash my hair. I actually went to beauty parlors as a young adult because I never learned how to wash my own hair as a child. I finally learned how to wash my hair in the shower while I was on tour with New York City Ballet. I had been terrified of getting soap in my eyes. I was extremely sheltered, so I had problems when I needed to be independent. I was frightened to go places on my own sometimes, and I am still a little bit that way. My parents were very protective, which made me a rather nervous person. I think this affected my acting and ballet careers.

Really, the saddest part of my childhood was that my parents did not get along well with each other. There was tension in the house. They were always bickering. I often wished they would get a divorce. Certain things stay in your mind as clear memories from childhood. Once, my father was upsetting my mother so much that she went into the kitchen, opened the cupboard and started smashing all the plates. She just kept throwing them on the floor, and she was crying hysterically. It really frightened me to see that kind of uncontrolled emotion. I also remember an argument between my parents at the dinner table. My father took the ketchup bottle and slammed it down, and the ketchup spurted up to the ceiling. Another time my father recorded our conversation at dinner surreptitiously. There was a fight that was recorded. On the recording, the first sound you hear is the very loud crunch of a carrot that set the tone for the whole fight. Once we discovered that he was audiotaping the dinner, everybody became much nicer to each other. It was, "Look what Daddy has done!"

My parents must have loved each other at least for some of their marriage. I think they were quite happy in my early childhood, when my father was playing with the Pittsburgh Symphony Orchestra and St. Louis Symphony Orchestra. There was a sense of community and belonging with those orchestras. A lot of the musicians had young families, and my mother hung out with the wives—most of the musicians were men. I have also seen film of my parents at the beach with my aunt and uncle, and they are having a good time. So even though my memory is of constant fighting, I know they had some fun together sometimes. However, with my father's depression, and my mother's disappointment that he did not make more money, it just set them up for problems. Probably my mother's constant criticism did not help my father's depression. My uncle offered my father work at one point, which he refused, and that made my mother mad, too.

I just used to pray that they would stop fighting. It was very difficult for me. I felt I needed to take sides, so I did. I mostly sided with my mother, and my father would get upset and say, "Why do you always take your mother's side?" I couldn't help that I felt my father was wrong, and that she was right, but maybe I didn't know the whole story. I do know that my mother could be very difficult at times, if not infuriating. When my father was on tour, I would be so excited when he was coming home; then when he was home, I would wish he would leave again because all they did was fight. I realize now that I was very angry with both of them for putting me in the middle of their dysfunctional relationship. Living in the midst of all that dysfunction must have had an effect on me. I recognize now that I had become quite a neurotic little girl. But my mother was the one who was always there for me. Despite her faults, she was the constant person in my life.

As I moved into high school, my mother backed off promoting my performance career. There were a couple of reasons for this. The first was that my uncle and aunt (on my mother's side, my cousin Barbara's parents) had always been negative about my career in the theater because, although they were excited and impressed that I was on the stage, they felt that I wasn't having a normal childhood. Ultimately, they made my mother feel guilty for constantly pushing me. The second reason was that my focus shifted almost exclusively to dance in high school. Although my mother was supportive of my dance career, she was never a "dance mom" as she had been a "stage mom."

These childhood experiences impacted my life significantly as I moved forward into the serious study of ballet.

Chapter 2

Becoming a Dancer

George Balanchine used to say, "Don't think, dear, just do." In my experience teaching in a college dance program, most dancers don't want to hear that. They want information from their teachers that will help them improve, but that also explains intellectually and anatomically what they need to do to activate their muscles. Someone once said to me that the students in college dance programs want to talk about dance more than they want actually to do it. I smiled when I heard that, but I think that comment reflects the negativity that was once associated with the level of training and student ability that existed in college dance programs in the 1960s and before. I know for a fact that Mr. Balanchine had little regard for these programs, which did not produce ballet dancers with any high degree of professional training or capability. That has all changed, as college dance programs today are training ballet dancers who can dance the Balanchine repertoire and who are getting jobs in ballet companies.

It is my theory that, if a ballet dancer has excellent foundational training and is a thinking, disciplined, and observant human being, that dancer can dance any kind of dance: modern, Broadway, jazz, and yes, contemporary ballet. But that foundational training must be there from the start, and it must encompass all the elements of technique found in classical ballet: adagio, turns, petit and grand allegro, beats, tours (aerial turns) for the men, and so on.

My training at the School of American Ballet (SAB), which is the official school of New York City Ballet and where I began study from the age of eight, was not analytical. I had only one teacher, Muriel Stuart, who mentioned anything at all about placement. The Russian teachers—Felia Doubrovska, Anatole Oboukhoff, Antonina Tumkovsky, and Pierre Vladimiroff—did not speak English well and consequently taught by demonstration and minimal explanation. We learned and improved by working hard, by imitation, and by watching the members of New York City Ballet when they would take class. We feared and respected our teachers and did not question their methods. This is my background, one of traditional training and respect for the aesthetics of a beautiful art form. Today the faculty at SAB is composed of dancers who were my contemporaries in the company, and these values continue to be taught there, representing the legacy of Balanchine's vision for a school and the roots of his training in Russia.

However, in some other institutions, there is what I consider to be a disturbing trend in ballet training. Dancers are encouraged to discard their ballet slippers and take class in socks to "feel" their feet and to disregard traditional dress code by wearing shorts, no tights, and loose-fitting practice clothes in order to feel more "comfortable" within their bodies. Ballet training, as I experienced it and as I teach it, is not meant to be comfortable. A certain freedom of movement can eventually come with having mastered the technique, but a "touchy-feely" approach to training is, in my opinion, no substitute for the hard work that traditional training requires.

Perhaps my attitude is old-fashioned. After all, this is the twenty-first century, and the face of ballet is changing. Modern dancers are choreographing for ballet companies, and ballet dancers need to adapt to new, experimental ways of working, which includes contemporary ballet. I see contemporary ballet as an often-interesting distortion of classical ballet vocabulary and positions, as opposed to Balanchine's aesthetic of neoclassic beauty, which adhered to the classical vocabulary. But each has its own place in the dance world. The difference is in the choreography and how it speaks to me. I would hate to see classical ballet training, as we have known it for hundreds of years, discarded and something less challenging put in its place. The stronger a dancer's technique, the more versatile that dancer will be.

As to my own training, from an early age outside of regular school, I studied ballet, tap, voice, and acting. However, although I was a professional child actor, I always really loved dance—it was my favorite. I was constantly dancing around the living room. My first dance class ex-

Dancing barefoot, circa 1950. Photo by Leo Rosenberg.

perience was when I was quite young, and it was basically interpretive dance. I have a vivid memory of a solo I performed. My teacher was Blanche Evan, who taught creative dance to children for twenty years in New York City. According to Iris Rifkin-Gainer, who also studied creative movement with Evan as a child, "we were guided to dance out themes which expressed our inner conflicts and those of the family and world around us."[1] This was the foundation of Evan's later work in dance therapy. She was a pioneer in this field and one of the original members of the American Dance Therapy Association.

My mom then took me to study with Nathalie Branitzka, who had studied with Agrippina Vaganova as a child in Russia and then danced with the Anna Pavlova company, Sergei Diaghilev's Ballets Russes, and Colonel W. de Basil's Ballet Russe company. She had a studio near Bloomingdale's, and it was up a steep and very narrow staircase, just like that song "At the Ballet" in *A Chorus Line*. She was a terrific teacher. My mother always managed to find the best teachers to give me lessons. I don't know how she found them, but she did.

Ballet became an increasingly strong focus. Of course, always wanting me to study with "the best," my mother took me to audition for George Balanchine's School of American Ballet (SAB). I was accepted and began classes there. For a short period, I left and went to Ballet Theatre (now called American Ballet Theatre) for lessons, but then came back to SAB, which, in those days, we called The American. I don't remember first meeting Balanchine because I knew him my whole childhood. I progressed through the children's classes and worked hard to be the best in my class. Balanchine was often around watching classes.

When I was thirteen or fourteen—and while I continued to be a daily afterschool SAB student—I auditioned for the High School of Performing Arts (HSPA), which specialized in drama, music, and dance. This was a New York City public school that was founded in 1947, with the first students attending in September of 1948. The original building was in the theater district, on West 46th Street. HSPA eventually merged with the High School of Music & Art to become Fiorello H. LaGuardia High School of Music & Art and Performing Arts, housed in a building just west of Lincoln Center. It may have been for financial reasons that my mother sent me to public school for high school. I am not positive. But HSPA ended up being a very good school for me.

I auditioned for the dance department and the acting department. I have no recollections of my audition for the acting department, but my dance solo was to music from the Broadway hit *Carousel*. I remember I had my hair loose. I started sitting on the floor, and then I danced barefoot. I was accepted into both dance and acting, so I needed to make a choice. I had been attending the Professional Children's School for eight years, and now I was going into unchartered waters: a new, public school without my elementary school friends, and no more showbiz (my acting career). HSPA did not encourage students to perform outside the school curriculum, plus I had braces on my teeth and was not attending auditions much anymore. I had a best friend named Marilyn Wasserman who was studying at the School of American Ballet with me. She had been accepted into the HSPA dance department also. I was nervous about entering this new environment and gravitated toward the dance program so that I could be with a friend. That was probably not the best reason for making such a decision, but looking back, I had wonderful teachers at HSPA, all of whom contributed to my excellent training and development as a dancer.

In choosing to major in dance, I began to focus almost entirely on ballet, and my acting career came to an end. My mother always felt that if I had stayed with acting, I would have had a much longer and more wonderful career. I know she was proud of my success as a ballet dancer, but she was much more invested in my career as an actor. It's certainly possible that I could have had a longer career in acting, depending on the success of that career along the way. For many, a career in ballet can end at only thirty or thirty-five years of age. But, despite preferring me to have an acting career, my mom never tried to discourage me from dancing. I don't think she was very interested in guiding my career in ballet, so my dance pursuits largely became my own endeavor, although my mom certainly wanted to see me dance solo roles, which I did. Of course, once she realized that my ultimate success as a ballet dancer depended on my remaining thin, she put the pressure on me in terms of weight. And yet, when I am often asked if I missed the acting part of my career, all I can say is that I loved everything I did: Broadway, television, being a chorus dancer in summer stock, a classical ballet dancer in one of the greatest companies in the world, and now a teacher. I feel extremely fortunate to have had and still have such a varied, exciting, and interesting career, and I can honestly say that I attribute much of my success to my mother who, despite her difficult disposition, provided emotional support, direction, guidance, and love.

When the dance department at HSPA suggested I major in modern dance, probably because I had not danced on pointe at my audition, I was surprised. I let them know soon enough that I wanted my focus to be ballet, although I really enjoyed the modern dance training I had. At HSPA, my teachers for modern dance were Stuart Hodes, Nancy Lang, Gertrude Shurr, Norman Walker, and David Wood. I loved them so much that I almost switched to being a modern major from being a ballet major! (I had big crushes on Norman Walker and Stuart Hodes). However, my training had been so predominantly in ballet that I decided to stick with a major in ballet. My ballet teachers were Harry Asmus, Ann Hutchinson (Guest), Bella Malinka, Nina Popova, and Olga Tavolga. I had Yurek Lazowsky for character dance. In my ballet classes, I was closest to Mr. Asmus. He was the first person to call me BJ, instead of Bettijane, and that became my nickname. Olga Tavolga was a very good teacher, very Russian, and a screamer, and I liked her classes; but I was closest to Mr. Asmus. I even took classes from him when I could, wherever he was teaching after school.

One of the places Mr. Asmus taught was the June Taylor dance studio, on West 56th Street and Broadway. One afternoon, I wore a black-and-white herringbone suit to the studio. I took it off to put on my dance clothes and left the suit and my shoes in the dressing room. When I came back, the suit and my shoes were gone! I called my mother, but I don't think she brought extra shoes and clothes for me to get home in. I can't even remember what I wore to get home, but I learned never to leave anything of value in the dressing room. Olga Tavolga and Mr. Asmus later opened a studio of their own on West 54th Street. I took classes from both of them there. I heard that they had an ongoing affair. Poor Mr. Asmus met an unfortunate fate many years later. It seems he was murdered in his home in Delaware, in 1977.[2] There were other teachers I took classes from, outside of SAB and HSPA. Through the years, these included Oliver McCool for tap; Matt Mattox and Luigi (Eugene Louis Faccuito) for jazz; and Robert Joffrey, Ludmilla Schollar, and Anatole Vilzak for ballet.

I don't remember performing any modern pieces at HSPA, but I did perform ballets. Mr. Asmus created a beautiful ballet, *Holberg Suite*, with music by Edvard Grieg, and he gave me a wonderful role. I also danced in a piece of his called *Ballinade*, in 1959, and a piece by Olga Tavolga,

High School of Performing Arts production program, circa 1960; I am the dancer at the bottom. Photographer unknown.

called *Reverie*, in 1960, my senior year. I won the dance award in my senior year, too.

HSPA was so enjoyable overall. We had "lunchtime dancing" in the downstairs lobby, when all of the 1950s rock 'n' roll songs came over the loudspeaker system, and the students danced. I was always afraid some boy would come up and ask me to dance. I felt so inexperienced. I didn't know how to talk to boys. I thought there was a special way you had to behave around them. So I think I must have sent out some negative vibes, and guys stayed away from me. But I danced the Lindy with my girlfriends, and it was great fun. I remember there were some kids in my class who were dating and got married: John Mineo and Kathy Hull. They were high school sweethearts. John Mineo did a lot of work on Broadway. I was involved in a panel discussion, on September 11, 2012, put together by the organization Dancers over 40. The panel was a group of Balanchine dancers, and we were interviewed by Candice Agree, Nancy Goldner, and Robert Greskovic. I am now a member of the organization, and I saw in a newsletter that John Mineo was one of the founding board members.

One of my friends in high school was Jane Kosminsky, who danced with the Paul Taylor Dance Company and now teaches Alexander Technique. I think about her often. Two of my best friends in high school were Marilyn Wasserman and Rita Schwartzberg, who were also dance majors. After school, we would all go to the Automat on West 44th Street and Broadway. Eating at the Automat was maybe not quite as fascinating to me as when I was a young child, but close! We would get those sticky buns and unravel the pastry as we ate them. They were so good with milk. Then we would take the subway uptown to 82nd Street and Broadway and take 4:30 class at SAB. Afterward, I went home to complete three or four hours of homework a night. It was a tough life, but I did it happily.

The original SAB studio (from 1933 to 1956) was on Madison Avenue, at East 59th Street.[3] I went there when I first auditioned at the age of eight, but it was the studio at Broadway and West 82nd Street where I had most of my training. Elise Reiman (1914–1993) was the only American-born teacher on the faculty. Then there was Muriel Stuart (1900–1991), who was born in England and had studied and danced with Anna Pavlova. I remember she was fond of pulling my arm forward to rest on her shoulder while she said, "tighten here [poking my rear end], pull up there and bring your upper body forward, dahling." As a result, my upper body placement was very forward and my ribs stuck out a bit. All the rest of the teachers were native Russians: Felia Doubrovska (1896–1981), Anatole Oboukhoff (1896–1962), Antonina Tumkovsky

(1905–2007), and Pierre Vladimiroff (1893–1970). The female teachers particularly were role models to me. The Russian women were very elegant in how they dressed and how they comported themselves. They were all old enough to be pre-Vaganova in terms of ballet style and technique, except for Tumkovsky, who was a little younger and trained and performed in Kiev, with postgraduate training with Agrippina Vaganova (1879–1951) at the Leningrad State School of Ballet.[4] For the others, Pavel Gerdt (1844–1917) was a major teacher in their training time period in St. Petersburg. Gerdt had been Balanchine's teacher, too.

All the teachers' classes were incredibly challenging, and I worked very hard, wanting to be recognized as the best in the class. I remember Valerie, a beautiful little blond girl with a turned-up nose and beautiful feet, who was Miss Stuart's favorite, and I wanted to be the favorite. Eventually, Valerie left the school, and I did become one of Miss Stuart's favorites. It wasn't long before all the teachers came to recognize my ability, musicality, and talent.

At SAB, we were taught a very strong foundational technique, which is what we would need if and when we joined the company. Nowadays, some teachers are teaching a more contemporary approach to ballet, but that is not at all how we were trained at SAB. Our training was traditional, with solid classical technique. That strong foundation then allowed us to go in many directions as professionals. The Balanchine style came on top of the classical technique, but his style wasn't taught at the school. We weren't doing the turned-in passés and other jazzy movements, for instance. You learned that when you joined the company. Because of our foundational training, we were able to adapt easily to Mr. B's focus on speed and the demands of his intricate choreography.

Tumkovsky taught very difficult classes when I was a child; and Vladimiroff, Oboukhoff, and Doubrovska also taught very difficult classes when I was older, into my high school years. Vladimiroff, who was married to Doubrovska, was a sweet, kind man, whose classes bored me to death because the combinations hardly ever varied. Oboukhoff, however, was one of my most influential teachers. He was a bit frightening because he would hit or tap you gently with his hand if you weren't doing what he wanted—for instance, if your knees weren't fully straight or your feet weren't fully pointed so that your Achilles tendon was hard. He was actually a shy man who did not have full command of the English language, and he would clear his throat in a loud, blustery way as a compensation for his difficulty with English. His classes were incredible and very hard. It was unbelievable training, and I think I was at my best from a technical standpoint when I was taking his classes. There is a lot to be said for fear of a teacher. He once gave a combination with quadruple pirouettes, and we were so afraid not to do them that we did them!

Mme. Doubrovska lent a classic elegance to her teaching, with her exquisite legs and feet, and just her very presence. She was the original Siren in Mr. B's *Prodigal Son* for Diaghilev's Ballets Russes. Her long, tapered legs defined that role. When she taught us, she wore beautiful silk dresses made especially for her, and she would hold her skirt up slightly as she demonstrated. Her legs and feet were mesmerizing.

Mme. Doubrovska had a little poodle, and she would bring the dog into the dance studio. One day Mr. B unexpectedly appeared at the top of the stairs. Meanwhile, the poodle had peed on the floor. Madame was so flustered and embarrassed that she spread her dance skirt and gracefully sat down on the pee to hide it from Mr. B. We all thought that was so amusing at the time. Madame had so much respect and love for Mr. B that she couldn't bear for him to see what her dog had done in the ballet studio.

Once when I was having lunch at the counter at the Schrafft's restaurant on West 82nd Street and Broadway, right next to SAB, Mme. Doubrovska came and sat next to me. She was so elegant and interested in me, and when she learned I was an only child, she remarked how unspoiled I was. I never forgot that. Oh, and Schrafft's had the best-ever coffee ice cream sodas and sundaes with hot fudge!

Schrafft's was very different from the Automat, which, of course, I also loved. It was a real restaurant as opposed to self-service. There was always a counter toward the front and a waitress service section in the back. And it had an air of elegance about it, with white tablecloths and napkins. In addition to ice cream treats, I remember their sandwiches; they served a tongue sandwich, something you don't often see on any menu today. In addition to the Schrafft's on West 82nd Street and Broadway, there was a Schrafft's on Broadway between West 107th and 108th Streets, around the corner from my apartment when I was growing up. My mother and I ate there frequently. We both were so busy with running from school to classes to auditions that often there was not time to cook at home.

In 1958, while in high school, I was an Angel in the televised *The Nutcracker* for CBS-TV's Playhouse 90, where Balanchine played Drosselmeyer. The Angels were all tall, older girls then, unlike the younger girls who are cast today. We were told to stand perfectly still while the other characters were dancing. Apparently, I was moving my eyes around to watch the dancing and was told not to do that. I guess it was distracting.

In those days, there was no Workshop performance series for advanced students at SAB, as there is each spring today, but I was privileged to be invited into the "special class" taught by Mme. Doubrovska. This class was for girls Mr. B felt showed particular promise and who were being groomed to join the company. And, indeed, it was special. We were told to wear only pointe shoes for class, not ballet slippers, and we were the envy of the school. Mr. B sometimes came and watched the class. Although I had not been on scholarship through my childhood, I was by this time. I don't know why I was not on scholarship from the beginning, except that my mother may never have asked.

The summer course was fantastic at SAB on West 82nd Street. Of course, there was no air-conditioning then, but each studio had big standing fans to circulate the air. One day, in Adagio class, Jacques d'Amboise taught, and he used me to demonstrate with him. He taught us part of *Afternoon of a Faun* (choreography by Jerome Robbins). There I was, being partnered by Jacques d'Amboise! I was wearing a little dance skirt, and, by the end of class, the skirt was in shreds from his strong hands manipulating me by the waist. But I didn't care—what an honor to be partnered by Jacques.

I attended many NYCB performances in the 1950s, and Jacques was one of the dancers I most loved to see. I admired his dancing completely. He was a real showman, a great partner, and tremendously exciting to watch. His height and good looks all contributed to his popularity, and Mr. B gave him wonderful roles to dance.

Melissa Hayden (Millie) was my favorite of all the ballerinas. She had acting ability as well as being such an incredible dancer. She embodied true artistry. I can remember rising to my feet at the end of her performances and yelling "Brava" at the top of my lungs. I even developed a crush on her and learned what perfume she wore—a man's fragrance called Zizanie.

Millie danced many classical roles, such as those in the Balanchine matinee favorites *Swan Lake*, *Firebird*, and *Western Symphony*, really showing her comedic talents in the second movement of *Western*. She managed to give her ballerina role a tongue-in-cheek humor, something I don't often see in the dancers who are performing it currently. They dance well, but the humor seems lost on them, and they take that section almost too seriously. Another ballet that allowed Millie to show her acting ability was *Illuminations* by Frederick Ashton. She danced the role of Profane Love wearing only one pointe shoe and her hair unbound. She was passionate and poetic, and I was so moved.

I remember Millie best, however, for her versatility in *The Still Point*, by Todd Bolender, and *Medea*, by Swedish choreographer Birgit Cullberg. In *The Still Point*, she is a woman alone, shunned by the two other couples. Then Jacques d'Amboise appears, and they fall in love. She danced with such dramatic poignancy and abandon she made me cry. In *Medea*, she kills her children. Her acting was as powerful as her dancing, and, again, I cried as the tragedy of the story unfolded pulling her toward its terrible conclusion. Mr. Balanchine appreciated Millie's gifts and gave her wonderful ballets to dance. Her role in the ground-breaking *Agon* and the flamboyant, technical lead in *Stars and Stripes* are just two examples of Balanchine's ability to create choreography that featured a dancer's specific strengths. Melissa Hayden will live on in my memory forever.

When I did not have a ticket, I used to sneak into the City Center theater to watch the NYCB performances. There were always a bunch of us from SAB who would try to get in. We would mingle with the crowd during intermission, and then we would run up to the second balcony and hope that we didn't get caught. Once I did get caught, and the ushers made me leave. They could be really nasty. The audience for NYCB in the 1950s was a very sophisticated crowd. I saw writer and artist Edward Gorey frequently attending performances, wearing his raccoon fur coat. He was tall and had a beard. Quite the character. He is well known for his animated credits for the PBS *Masterpiece Mystery!* series.

One day in 1961, Count Raymundo de Larrain (a Chilean decorator, set designer, and photographer) came to SAB and picked a handful of girls to perform at a gala society ball, featuring French ballerina Violette Verdy and Danish dancer Erik Bruhn, at the Waldorf Astoria. Wearing thirty-pound headdresses, made largely of feathers, we were lifted and carried around in unusual positions by our male partners. I was always afraid of being dropped—very scary, but memorable.

In costume for the Count Raymundo de Larrain production *The Snow Bird* at the Waldorf Astoria, 1961. Photographer unknown.

Chapter 3

New York City Ballet, Corps de Ballet

When I graduated from high school in 1960, I thought I would get into New York City Ballet right away. I had studied at George Balanchine's School of American Ballet from the age of eight through my childhood and teen years. I knew Mr. Balanchine had been watching my progress since I was in the children's division, and I knew that all the teachers thought highly of me. However, the year I graduated high school, Rosemary Dunleavy (who would become assistant ballet mistress in 1971 and ballet mistress in 1983) and Susan Kenniff, both my classmates at SAB, were immediately invited to join the company, and I was not. I was very disappointed. I had always assumed I would get into NYCB, but after I was passed over that year, some slight doubts started to creep in, plus I had gained some weight. I continued to work hard, taking my classes at SAB, and hoping for the best; however, I also started taking courses at Hunter College at my mother's suggestion. She had graduated from Hunter College herself.

Betty Cage, NYCB company manager, sent me a letter in the spring of 1961 saying that, although I was not being asked to apprentice for the spring season, they would like me to become an apprentice in the fall. Because the letter was no guarantee and I wanted to make some money, I auditioned for summer stock and landed a job in a theater company in Framingham, Massachusetts. At that point, June 8, 1961, I went to the director of SAB to let her know I would not be attending the summer course because I had signed a contract to dance in a summer stock production. Before I could begin to tell her, she said to me in her deep Russian-accented voice: "Mr. Balanchine would like to know if you would care to join the company on its tour to California this summer?" Would I care to? I couldn't believe it! "You may go over to City Center and sign your contract," she said abruptly. This was a moment in time that defined the rest of my life.

I left her office in a daze, and after calling my mother to tell her my good news, I took the bus from SAB, on Broadway at West 82nd Street, to City Center's stage door, on West 56th Street, where I took the elevator to the eighth floor, signed my contract, and was told that the tour would begin in July and would include Los Angeles, San Francisco, Vancouver, British Columbia (the company's Canadian debut),[1] and Evanston, Illinois. I was thrilled! Not only was this finally NYCB for me but this would also be my first trip to the West Coast. However, I needed to get out of my summer stock contract. I took a Greyhound bus to Framingham, Massachusetts, found the theater, and signed the necessary papers to release me from my contract. Everyone in the stock company was thrilled for me and wished me well.

When I was asked to join the company, of course I stopped taking classes at Hunter. (I would eventually complete my degree through Empire State College). I know people dance with the company today and take a few courses each semester, too, but it just wasn't done in my day. Getting into NYCB was a dream turned reality, and it was my complete and utter priority. I can still "feel" that thrill of knowing I had made it after all my years of hard work.

My mom was very proud that I had gotten into the company. She always came to see everything I was in, although she would sometimes say, "Well, which one were you? Because you all look alike. You are all blond, and with the hair back, you all look the same." And I'd say, "Gee, thanks Mom. Were you really there?" And she'd say, "Yes, but which one were you?" I forgive her. In truth, even though we all wore our hair the same, and there were many blond female dancers, our bodies were not replicas of one another. It seems to me that as SAB has become more selective as to whom they accept, the result is that the current women in the company have a uniform look that is different from the more varied look in my day.

My name was officially Bettijane Sills when I joined the company in 1961, but people called me BJ, except for Mr. B, who always called me J and B. I think it was a reference to the scotch whiskey by that name. My mother and I had come up with "Sills" eventually, after all the variations of Siegel, my actual family name. Everybody asked me if I was related to Beverly Sills, and they still do, but we are not related, and that's not her real name either. She was born Belle Miriam Silverman. One funny thing happened regarding our common last name: From 1964 on, New York City Ballet and New York City Opera used to share the New York State Theater. The Opera would be rehearsing while we were performing. One week, I received an overtime check for $4.95, and it was in an envelope that said B. Sills. Beverly Sills found it at the switchboard of the State Theater by the stage door. She opened it before she realized it wasn't hers, then she wrote on the envelope, "Opened by mistake," and enclosed a note that said: "Dear B. Sills, You need a raise." She signed the note: B. Sills. Leonard Lyons wrote it up for his column in the *New York Post!*[2]

The roster of female principal dancers when I joined the company included Diana Adams, Melissa Hayden, Jillana, Patricia Wilde, and Violette Verdy. I was in awe of Melissa Hayden. She exemplified all I wanted to be as a dancer. And Violette was so sweet, which showed through in her dancing. She was also extremely musical and remarkably turned-out, which we marveled at. (Turn-out is the outward rotation of the legs in the hip socket, which allows for greater freedom of leg movement and gives a stylistic definition to classical movement.)

A very young Patricia McBride was starting to get roles. We called her "little Patty" at SAB when we were all students. She had the perfect ballerina face: large features, beautiful eyes, which make-up enhanced—a great stage face. Somehow, she never hit an awkward position when she danced. From whatever angle you looked at her, there was something lovely to see. She was so nice to everyone that no one ever begrudged her the roles Mr. B gave her. I once told her I was nervous about a certain role I was going to dance, and she said to me in her little, high voice, "Don't worry, BJ. You'll be fine."

By the time I joined the company, Mr. B's wife and muse Tanaquil Le Clercq had already become disabled from polio and was in a wheelchair, but she and Mr. B were still married. Occasionally, we would hear that she was coming to the ballet, but she never came backstage, or, if she did, I don't remember seeing her. For me, she was a distant figure and a reminder of that frightening time in the 1950s when polio had not yet been eradicated. I was shocked later on when Balanchine divorced her so that he could marry Suzanne Farrell, which, of course, didn't go as he had planned.

When I first joined the company, in 1961, Mr. B held a seminar for teachers from around the country, and several of the NYCB dancers participated, including me. These seminars were held at the School of American Ballet on 82nd Street and Broadway. In the book *Balanchine Teaching*, Nancy Lassalle and Suki Schorer give some background information:

> In 1960, at the instigation of W. McNeil Lowry, the Program Director at the Ford Foundation, a grant was given to Ballet Society enabling the School of American Ballet to survey the quality of American ballet instruction. This survey sets the backdrop against which the Teachers' Seminars, eight in all, were given.[3]

Ms. Lassalle photographed the second Teachers' Seminar, which took place over two days in 1961. This was the one I took. In the photographs in Ms. Lassalle's book, one can see Mr. B demonstrating the power of plié (bend of the knees), use of épaulement (use of head, neck, and shoulders), and the opening of the hip to allow the leg to rise behind the dancer in arabesque.

I also started taking company class, which began at 10 or 10:30 a.m. and was taught by Mr. B. The classes were two hours long, and since Mr. B never watched the clock, sometimes longer. His energy seemed boundless. He usually wore his Western shirt, a string tie, and street shoes or sometimes laced jazz shoes. He didn't always demonstrate full out, but often he did. Sometimes he used his hands to show the combinations. He would jump a little too, say, in a glissade assemblé. He didn't generally use other people to demonstrate. If a dancer was doing something particularly well, he might say—"like that." I wish I had had the foresight to write down his combinations, but alas, it never occurred to me at the time.

I was very nervous my first day of company class, afraid that I would call attention to myself, but Mr. B was so inspiring to watch that my self-consciousness was soon forgotten. Instead, I found myself trying to absorb everything he said—his corrections, his little anecdotes, his jokes. I felt so honored to be part of his world. What he said to me, and what he would say to dancers when he first took them into the company, was: "Now I'm going to teach you how to dance," because he wanted to add to what we already knew. We had the foundation—we had been trained with a very strong classical Russian technique. And you could see the Russian underpinnings in what he was doing—Mr. B had had strict Russian training just as we did. At SAB, we were studying with dancers he had known in Russia. But once we entered the company, he needed to teach us more, so that we would be prepared to perform his choreography the way he wanted it done—with speed, clarity, and athleticism. In his classes, he built on that, although we didn't do anything that was actually part of his choreography.

You really had to give yourself a good warm-up before Mr. B's class, because you wouldn't necessarily get fully warm from it. It was kind of like his laboratory. He was not interested in warming us up slowly. Classes began with a short barre. Grand pliés (deep knee bends) were mostly in two counts: one count down, one count up. I always felt he wanted to get them out of the way so as to move along to what really interested him. We would start out with excruciatingly slow tendus, with emphasis on the toe in absolute line with the belly button to the front and small of the back behind. Then, we would build up speed. Sometimes he gave exercises that were so unbelievably fast that there was practically no way to execute them without struggling to control our legs. Mr. B used to say that the body wants to go to sleep, and we needed to fight against that. He saw that we American dancers in general had great energy, and he would push us to the nth degree. "What are you waiting for dear? You might be hit by a truck tomorrow. Do it now. There is only today." I realized much later, when I began to teach, how the process of working beyond the comfort zone would develop strength and the ability to move quickly or slowly. Mr. B also wanted everyone to move bigger—small dancers to move bigger, and tall dancers to move bigger. And we didn't know we could do it, and then we did.

We spent much time standing in the center trying to imitate Balanchine's mesmerizing hands and port de bras (carriage of the arms). Sometimes he would get so focused on hands and port de bras that we didn't get through a full class. He would patiently show us what he wanted the hands to look like. He was not interested in "soft hands." The idea that ballet dancers should have "soft" hands was a myth. He did not want to see them limp and lifeless. Softness was an illusion. Our hands could *look* soft, but in reality they were held with strength and shape. He liked to see fingers and space between the fingers, so that the hand was held expressively and exquisitely, but also strongly. The thumbs needed to be visible as long as we did not appear to be hitchhiking, and the pinky finger needed to have a delicate crook to it, as if we were holding a teacup.

My first year, since I was new in the company, Mr. B spent quite a bit of time correcting me. One day, early on in my time with the company, he stood in front of me trying to get me to understand what he wanted with the hands. Every time I tried he would say "No, dear." This went on for some time with everyone watching, and all he would say was "No, dear." I started to panic. Finally he said, "You will get it, dear," and he walked away, and the class continued. He didn't try to discourage people. He had enormous patience. He thought eventually we would understand, and we did.

Most days, we did tendus and pirouettes, adagio, and small and big jumps across the floor. Musicality was continually stressed. For arabesque, we lengthened our fingers as if reaching for a diamond ring or whatever we wanted most. Nothing about our bodies was stationary as we reached with the front arm, back arm, and foot to elongate our line. He also liked the torso as upright as possible in an arabesque. He would put his hand under your chin to keep you from pushing the torso forward and ask you to lift your leg. It created a shape more perpendicular than curved. The hip was never raised when the leg was extended in arabesque, but it was open to permit maximum rotation and line. There was no twisting of the upper body.

When Mr. B focused on jumps, he would tell us to "jump like pussycat"—you don't see the preparation but suddenly you are up there. (He had a cat named Mourka that he loved.) Much has already been written about the misconception that Balanchine didn't want us to put our heels down. Often, he would want us to plié so deeply that the heels would come up, but I don't recall that we ever were asked to land from a jump with our heels off the floor. So much of his choreography was so fast that in order to represent his material with the requisite lightness, sometimes the heels couldn't come down. He saw how Scottish dancers were so light on their feet and used that idea. So you might land with your heels slightly up from a jump before lowering the heels. He was looking for speed and lightness.

Mr. B was always trying to make a movement more beautiful. He used to stand in front of a dancer in class and say, "Can you be pretty, dear?" The look could become more important than the physical principles of how to do the movement. For instance, Mr. B demanded extreme turn-out and really was not interested in how we got there. Maybe our hips were not squared off; he didn't seem to care as long as the working leg was turned-out. I suppose those of us who had been trained to turn-out properly had fewer knee and hip problems later.

At one point, Mr. B separated the women and the men in class. John Taras taught the men, and Mr. B taught the women. I do remember, when the classes were combined, that he sometimes focused more on the women than the men. He had respect for the men and created some wonderful male roles, but I remember more about how he related to the women.

All the women took company class on pointe, not in ballet slippers. It just was what was done. It gave you a real sense of the shoe being part of you, an extension of the line and integral to the technique. When I first joined the company, I wore Selva brand pointe shoes, a boxy shoe (long since gone from the scene). Diana Adams suggested that I switch to something else. She acted as Mr. B's spokesperson. She called him "the Boss." So, I switched to Capezio's for a short time, and then Mr. B announced he wanted us to wear Freed's. He was particularly bothered by the noise the other shoes made in a ballet such as *Serenade*, with so much running. I wore Freed's pointe shoes from then on. Depending on how many ballets I was dancing in a given week, I requested as many pairs of pointe shoes as I thought I needed—sometimes eight pairs a week, sometimes fewer. And it also depended on the ballets—did I need harder shoes or softer shoes, in other words could I wear the shoes more than once? For *Concerto Barocco*, I needed hard shoes because of the hops on pointe and the amount of time on stage. In those days, there were only Capezio, Freed, and Selva. Now there are many different shoes from different makers. When I was a student, pointe shoes cost $8.00 a pair. Now it's more like $80.00!

Some of the dancers preferred not to take Mr. B's class: At different points in time, they included Gelsey Kirkland, Peter Martins, and Edward Villella. They didn't really get punished per se, but Mr. B did not like the fact that they were not taking his class. The dancers who skipped Mr. B's class often took Stanley Williams's class at SAB. Stanley had been trained at the Royal Danish School of Ballet in Copenhagen, and then was a principal dancer with the Royal Danish Ballet. Mr. B invited him to teach at the School of American Ballet in 1964; he was teaching in the Bournonville tradition with his own take on that. Not only NYCB dancers took his classes but also "outside" dancers, like Rudolf Nureyev and Erik Bruhn. Erik Bruhn was a guest artist with NYCB in the early 1960s. I have a wonderful memory of holding Erik's hand in a curtain call and feeling thrilled to be next to this superstar. He was so beautiful.

After company class ended, there were rehearsals throughout the day, whether we were in performance season or not. When I joined the company, I was first asked to learn *Swan Lake*, *Western Symphony*, and *Symphony in C*. Each rehearsal was an hour long, and by the end of the day, my head was swimming. How was I going to remember all those steps? I wrote them down as best I could as a tool to help me remember. But I found out that I was a quick study, which would be useful to the company and my career in the future. I learned quickly and retained choreography well, and the company came to rely on me in emergencies. I was often "thrown" into a ballet after barely an hour's rehearsal, and I became an expert at following the girl in front of me. As one example, shortly after I had been made a soloist, our ballet mistress Francia Russell came into my dressing room after I had just finished *Allegro Brillante*. Another dancer was sick or injured, and she needed me to do my old *Stars and Stripes* corps de ballet part immediately. I was exhausted, but I jumped into the costume and ran on stage.

Before we left for California, that summer of 1961, the company performed as part of the Empire State Festival at Bear Mountain from July 13 to 19.[4] The performances were funded by the first grant given to a

Coming down the center in the "The Waltz" from *Swan Lake*, circa 1961. Photo by Fred Fehl. Photo courtesy Gabriel Pinski.

performing arts organization by the New York State Council on the Arts, which itself was brand new.[5] Finally, I was ready for my first *Swan Lake*. This was my debut with the company. In preparation for the performance, the older girls helped me with my hair for *Swan Lake* showing me how to "wing" it with spit curls pinned next to my ears and then pulling my hair over the spit curls and fastening it with hairpins. No one really showed me how to apply makeup; I just watched the other girls and experimented to see what type of eyeliner and shading suited my face. At first, I drew funny triangles above my eyes with colored eye shadow, and the girls probably thought I was weird, or that I knew something they didn't, but the triangles were only my translation of what I thought I saw the other dancers doing. I soon changed that to a more normal

Symphony in C, 1965. David Richardson and me in front. Photo by Martha Swope ©Billy Rose Theatre Division, The New York Public Library for the Performing Arts.

look after studying the way the other dancers applied their eye shadow. Brown shadow looked best on me and, applied in the crease between my eye and brow, made my eyes look more deep-set.

I was nervous and felt my legs shaking as I made my first entrance, but soon my nervousness was replaced by a feeling of exhilaration. Here I was, dancing to glorious music in a beautiful white costume, and I felt free. Perhaps this is why actors must act, singers must sing, and dancers must dance. To be able to feel this incredible sense of freedom within a structured framework is a compelling thing. One of the wonderful aspects of Mr. B's choreography was that everyone danced a lot, even the corps de ballet. That is part of what made his ballets so glorious to dance. You weren't ever just stuck as a kind of scenery in a tutu. In addition to *Swan Lake*, I probably also danced in *Western Symphony* and as a "Horn" in *Fanfare* (by Jerome Robbins), which were some of my first roles. We performed in a big tent held up by thick ropes, and I scraped my shin very badly on one of the ropes holding up the tent.

We went by train to California (San Francisco and then Los Angeles), and my mother accompanied me. Overprotective as always, she wanted to come, and I had never been on my own before, so I guess I was glad she was there. The first night on the train I was so excited I couldn't sleep, so I wandered around the sleeping car looking for company. Most of the other new girls were awake, too, so we stayed up all night talking.

Lunch in the dining car of the train was fun. Patricia Neary (who was a friend of mine), my mother, and I ate together one day. Pat ordered a chef's salad, and what did she find at the bottom of her bowl? A dead moth. We were hysterical! We stopped in Needles, California, to get off the train and stretch our legs. It had to have been 110 degrees. It was like stepping into an oven, certainly memorable.

Once we arrived in Los Angeles, the routine of touring was established. As at home, there would be class every morning followed by rehearsals for that evening's performance. I had written down the steps I was to perform in *Swan Lake* and rehearsed by myself in the hotel room I shared with my mother. We stayed at the Blair House. There would be various times throughout the day when we could grab a snack and a few hours to rest back at the hotel. Dinner in the dining room there was the first time I had ever eaten salad before my meal. My mother always served salad with the meal. I remember feeling so healthy.

If we had a few hours before going back to the theater, we would go to the pool and sit in the sun. With the sun, pool, and good food, it was so relaxing that it was difficult to "rev" myself up to dance. But on this tour, I learned the necessity of "doing a barre" before each performance even though I had had a class in the morning and rehearsal most of the day. Warming up the muscles carefully before a performance prevents injury and cramping. Getting sunburned or tanned was frowned upon by Mr. B because we needed to look alabaster under the blue lights for *Serenade* and *Swan Lake*. But of course, some of us did get sunburned, which made us look purple, so we wore white body makeup for these ballets.

In Los Angeles, outside the Blair House, 1961. Photo by Ruth Siegel.

We performed at the historic Greek Theatre, an outdoor venue, in Los Angeles. One ballet I particularly remember performing is *The Nutcracker*. How odd to be dancing a Christmas ballet in the summer and outdoors in the summer heat! In addition, *Electronics*, Mr. B's experiment with electronic music by Remi Gassmann and Oskar Sala, was on the program. I learned a part in this ballet very quickly to replace another dancer, and I performed it here in the Greek Theatre. The costumes went right along with the electronic score—we wore white leotards and tights with white pointe shoes and silver tinsel ponytails. Mr. B insisted the music be played at deafening decibel levels, and people in the surrounding communities complained. Someone said the music was so loud, it caused an avalanche! Mr. B refused to lower the volume. NYCB tours to California became an annual event for several years.

On the way back east from California, we performed at the Ravinia

Festival in Highland Park, Illinois (near Chicago). Ravinia is the summer home of the Chicago Symphony Orchestra and the oldest outdoor music festival in North America.[6] There were no wings to speak of (the curtained areas on the sides of a performance space that facilitate entrances and exits), and that made dancing the ballets with larger casts a bit complicated. We had to time our entrances carefully, so we were not waiting long in the very small wing space. But I loved performing there. How beautifully the Chicago Symphony Orchestra played all the ballets. We stayed in Evanston, Illinois, and I did some shopping at Marshall Field's department store.

Back in New York, my life settled into a rhythm of classes, rehearsals, and performances. On days when we had a matinee and evening performance, I often went for dinner to the Horn & Hardart, which was near City Center where we were performing at that time. This Horn & Hardart was a retail restaurant with only counter service at this point (no Automat). I always ordered the Salisbury steak or spaghetti with red sauce, my two favorite meals from when I was a child.

Some evenings I would sit in the lobby of the Wellington Hotel (on Seventh Avenue and West 55th Street), also near City Center, while I was waiting for a friend to meet me to go to dinner. One time I was sitting in the lobby on one of the comfortable couches, and someone from the hotel staff came up to me and asked me what I was doing there. I think they thought I was a hooker doing business! I hastened to explain that I was meeting a friend. I stopped sitting in the lobby of the Wellington Hotel after that.

A couple of very significant dancers who joined NYCB shortly after me, were Marnee Morris and Suzanne Farrell. Mr. B used to say he wanted the dancers to have high school diplomas before he took them into the company, but neither of them had one yet. Marnee became a student at SAB in 1959 when she was thirteen and joined the company just two years later.[7] Marnee's mother was ever-present and accompanied us on tour. Of course, Marnee was a child, and other mothers, including my own, also toured with us at times.

I remember that Marnee had the most beautiful skin. I always struggled with acne and had to be diligent about cleaning my face well. I roomed with her once on tour, and she went to bed with her stage makeup on, which I could never do. Nothing affected her beautiful skin. I was so jealous of that. Marnee also had a very womanly figure. She was not small-breasted like many ballet dancers, and she had long, slender legs with clear muscle definition. Everything about her was in proportion, and she was, in addition, a beautiful dancer. Everything Mr. B gave her to dance, she danced well. Mr. B soon promoted her to the rank of soloist, and she was given principal roles. She was an exceptional turner, so he created the turning girl lead for her in *Who Cares?* (among other roles). She was the second violin in *Concerto Barocco*, paired with Suzanne Farrell, and her Dewdrop in *The Nutcracker* was stupendous. Although she was known for her turns, she was extremely musical, could jump well, and looked great in short tutus with those tapered legs.

But after she left NYCB, she went through some very hard times. At one point she was living in a halfway house in South Dakota.[8] Once, after I had left the company and was visiting Deni Lamont (who had stopped dancing and was working for the company administratively), Marnee called him from the switchboard at the stage door. She needed money, and Deni had been helping her out. I don't presume to be clairvoyant, but I always felt there was something tragic about Marnee. She passed away in 2011.[9]

Suzanne Farrell joined NYCB in the fall of 1961. She had just turned sixteen in August. Balanchine became obsessed with the way she moved, and he focused much of his choreographic energy on her. When you follow his personal life and career, you can see that his wives were, to a one, his "muses of the moment," although this did not work out with Suzanne. His extraordinary attention to her annoyed many of the older ballerinas, and there was considerable jealousy of her among the soloists as well. He catered to her injuries, so, for instance, since she had bad knees, we didn't do grand pliés in company class because she couldn't do them without pain. It became even more necessary to warm yourself up before company class, and some dancers came to resent this seeming lack of concern for the rest of us as long as Suzanne was comfortable.

While it is true many dancers were very jealous of Suzanne, I was not. When Balanchine began to focus so much attention on Suzanne, I didn't feel that I received less attention than before, although probably some of the principal dancers felt that way. I think Millie (Melissa Hayden) may have felt neglected, but she also probably danced a little beyond her prime. It is better to go out in a blaze of glory than have people saying you should have retired a year ago. But, at the same time, I appreciate how difficult it is to stop dancing and no longer perform. It is so much a part of your identity.

If Mr. B had been choreographing for me and suddenly stopped, maybe I would have felt differently. But despite the overwhelming attention paid to Suzanne, Mr. B still created ballets and roles for other dancers. He continued to appreciate the people who worked hard and gave everything on stage, and I was one of those people. And I think about Patricia McBride—he created lovely things for her even though he was obsessed with Suzanne. I honestly don't know how, or if, I would have been able to handle the kind of attention Mr. B paid to Suzanne. Perhaps I was relieved not to be in her position, which may explain my lack of jealousy.

I always liked Suzanne very much, and we had a good relationship. She had this cool, remote quality about her coupled with a dry sense of humor, and she was always friendly to me. We were never close—after all, she was in a very difficult position as Balanchine's muse of the moment. But I believe that she spoke positively about me to Mr. B when they were watching from the wings, and this may have influenced casting.

My early career progressed well and quite quickly. I was dancing four ballets practically every night through the fall season and rehearsing strenuously during the day. For every ballet I learned, I would buy the recording of it (LPs at this time) and listen to the music over and over again in my apartment. I was completely immersed in my world and determined to perform every ballet the best that I possibly could.

One of the ballets I learned and performed soon after I joined the company was *The Figure in the Carpet* (1960), which we referred to as "Bug in the Rug." The ballet was inspired by the ornate patterns found in Persian carpets.[10] I was put into the "Sands" section with costumes like the long *Serenade* dresses, only in beige. It was beautiful choreography, traveling like the wind all over the stage. The ballet was soon dropped from the repertoire. In later years, there was a push to revive it, but there was no complete film or video of it, and not enough original cast members could remember it, so it was lost forever.

I was in the premiere of Mr. B's new ballet *Raymonda Variations* (originally titled *Valses et Variations*) on December 7, 1961, as a member of the corps. Clement Crisp of London's *Financial Times* described *Raymonda Variations* in glowing terms after one of our performances at Covent Garden, London, in 1965. He noted that it has the look of an excerpt from "some lost St. Petersburg masterpiece," however Balanchine treats "the score with a freedom and a subtlety that were unthinkable 50 years ago . . . giving new interest to the standard academic vocabulary."[11]

As it happens, I was not originally called to learn the ballet from the first rehearsal. The names of the dancers went up on the rehearsal callboard, and my name was not there. I was upset because all the girls who were called were my contemporaries. I got up the courage to ask John Taras why I wasn't called, and he said he had made a mistake and had accidentally left my name off the list. I was so glad I had asked him. He made me an understudy and told me to learn Leslie Ruchala's place. As luck would have it, Leslie soon announced that she was getting married and was leaving the company, so I went right into her spot. The rehearsals were great fun—the Glazunov music was glorious, as was the choreography. Eventually, I performed Carol Sumner's variation (I followed her in quite a few roles), and I performed two other variations, too: the one originally choreographed for Suki Schorer and the one for Victoria Simon. Victoria's had hops on pointe traveling across the stage. I enjoyed all three, but my favorite was Carol Sumner's.

As my life in the company continued, I was asked to learn many new roles in previously choreographed ballets, and, through this, became aware of the unfairness that is bound to exist in an organization governed solely by one man. Even though there was a board of directors and Lincoln Kirstein was the general director, Mr. B was clearly in charge of artistic matters. As an example, early in my career, I was cast in the corps of *Divertimento No. 15*, a "prestige" ballet. Another older dancer was the understudy waiting her turn, and I was cast over her. I knew she was terribly upset, and although I was elated to have been cast, I felt bad for her.

There was just an unspoken understanding that certain ballets were

Raymonda Variations, circa 1961. *From left to right*: Carol Sumner, Gail Crisa, and me. Photo by Fred Fehl. Photo courtesy Gabriel Pinski.

considered "prestige," and it was somewhat unusual for a new company member to be cast in them. *Divertimento No. 15* was one, along with *Concerto Barocco, Serenade, Allegro Brillante,* and *Agon.* These ballets seemed more important than the old warhorse favorites like *Swan Lake, Firebird,* and *Western Symphony* that the company always scheduled for matinees. Balanchine cared very much about the casting of the prestige ballets. In *Allegro,* the four couples were basically soloists whose execution of the choreography had to be danced with only the utmost energy, technical precision, and musicality. In *Barocco,* the same was true of the eight corps members who represented the orchestra in concert with the principal women who represented the two violins. *Serenade* allowed us

Agon, 1966. I am the furthest upstage. Photo by Martha Swope ©Billy Rose Theatre Division, The New York Public Library for the Performing Arts.

to move with complete joy and freedom within a large ensemble. The four corps women in *Agon* were integral to the structure of the ballet and needed to understand the mathematics of the music.

I knew one had to be considered a special dancer to get cast in those prestige ballets, and I was fairly quickly cast in all three. I had a small notice in a *New York Times* review of *Agon*, in 1962, praising the principal dancers as well as "the four minor figures—Diana [*sic*] Consoer, Marlene Mesavage, Bettijane Sills, and Victoria Simon" as being "all that could be desired."[12] I was told that Mr. B must like my dancing to cast me in these ballets. Naturally, I felt uncomfortable. I knew my colleagues resented me and were jealous, so I went out of my way to be quiet about my bit of good fortune. The competition at NYCB was always intense and was tied up in wanting Mr. B's attention. He was a father figure to all of us and perhaps particularly to the dancers who did not have their biological fathers in their lives as strong guiding figures.

I saw that casting was not usually a question of one's length of time in the company but rather of whether Mr. B felt one dancer was more suited to a certain role than another. This rejection of the rule of seniority was one of the ways in which Mr. B departed from the tradition of the ballet world. If you were right for a role, in his eyes, you would get to dance that role, whether in the corps or soloist or principal. This benefited me very much in my early career and less so later.

Related to that idea, around 1964, in an attempt to institute democracy in the company, Mr. B insisted on listing all the dancers alphabetically in the program—no more designations as principal, soloist, or corps de ballet. This was partly his response to what he considered temperamental "diva" behavior from some of the principal dancers, but it was only short-lived, because even with all the dancers listed alphabetically, there were still stars and those who stood out.

As a new company member, I found myself very anxious to be accepted and liked by the older members of the company, and I welcomed any corrections or help they would offer. I also noticed some of the older girls seemed very bitter and disillusioned about the company, and I hoped that I wouldn't suffer the same fate. I was so young and so excited. It was hard to take in the emotional and psychological states of dancers whose careers had maybe not been all that they had hoped for.

Around this time, I started receiving large, beautiful bouquets of flowers accompanied by an unsigned card that said something simple like "an admirer." I subsequently found out the flowers were from another dancer's husband. It was kind of exciting and romantic while it was happening, but awkward once I knew who was sending the flowers!

During my second year with the company, I was cast in Mr. B's first original full-length ballet, *A Midsummer Night's Dream*, which premiered on January 17, 1962.

I was cast as a Fairy, part of Titania's retinue, in Act I, and in the Divertissement in Act II. The original Titania was to be Diana Adams, but Melissa Hayden danced it in the première. Rehearsals for the Fairy sections

A Midsummer Night's Dream, 1962. I am standing at the back on the far left. Photo by Fred Fehl. Photo courtesy Gabriel Pinski.

A Midsummer Night's Dream, 1962. I am third from the right. Notice the funny wigs that we called Brillo pads. Photo by Fred Fehl. Photo courtesy Gabriel Pinski.

were fun, and Mr. B worked quickly, as usual. In Act I, the Fairies were to look like Botticelli maidens. We wore diaphanous pink flowing dresses that revealed the body beneath. We were told "no bras," and I admit to being a little shocked that the costumes were see-through. Janet Reed, ballet mistress at the time, told me to wear Band-Aids on my nipples if I was concerned, but no bra. We also wore pink wigs that had curls to complete the Botticelli look. Eventually the wigs were discarded, and we were allowed to fix our own hair.

In Act II, the Divertissement was part of the wedding scene. In this section, we were the entertainment of the court, hearkening back to the storyline and choreographic architecture of classical ballets such as *The Sleeping Beauty*. This was not something you see very often in Mr. B's choreography. The Divertissement was considerably difficult choreographically. I was cast with Deni Lamont as one of the six solo couples in this section, which featured Violette Verdy and Conrad Ludlow. The original costumes were tutus for the women, also with pink wigs, which looked like Brillo pads, so that's what we called them. In the original version of the dance, after the Pas de Deux, there was a separate section for the six women followed by a dance for the six men (a fugue) and then the Finale. Mr. B eventually cut the women's dance, probably to shorten things. The costumes were changed; the wigs were eliminated; and we wore little hats.

I have vivid memories of rehearsals for the Divertissement. I was fairly new in the company, and this was a plum role to have been given. I believe it was John Taras who cast me, but Mr. B would have to have approved. My partner Deni was so much fun to work with and very helpful. One step, in particular, gave me trouble: a promenade in arabesque holding Deni's hand with my left hand. I am right-handed, so this was a little hard for me. Deni and I kept falling out of it. Mr. B stood in front of me, and I just got more nervous and frustrated, but then he said, "You'll get it, dear," and he walked away. I was so grateful, and yes, I did eventually get it, but Deni and I practiced that promenade before every performance.

Walter Terry was quite enamored of *A Midsummer Night's Dream*, writing:

> The beauties of David Hays' scenery and the marvels of Barbara Karinska's costumes are a major aspect of this spectacle-ballet but they by no means outshine the choreographic wonders that George Balanchine has wrought, especially in Act I. For in Act I alone, Mr. Balanchine has given us in dance form the entire plot, along with the major and complex sub-plots, of the Shakespeare drama. And he has worked this magic not by using pantomime but through dancing itself coupled with danced gesture.[13]

We filmed the full-length ballet at a sound stage in Manhattan, in the West 50s, in 1966. By this time, Mr. B was in the throes of love for Suzanne Farrell. She danced the role of Titania, and there were a number of close-ups of her face. One day, she appeared wearing a small necklace, a delicate little pearl on a gold chain, given to her by Mr. B. She wore it in the film. It was all the talk.

A Midsummer Night's Dream movie, 1966. *On front row from left to right*: Sara Leland, Marnee Morris, Carol Sumner, and me. Photo by Martha Swope ©Billy Rose Theatre Division, The New York Public Library for the Performing Arts.

completed, and that was the only time I ever saw the complete film. It was eventually released in theaters in 1967, and it can now be seen at the Jerome Robbins Dance Division of the New York Public Library for the Performing Arts. It is a memorable piece of dance history.

In 1962, I was also in the original *Noah and the Flood*. This work was conceived and developed by Igor Stravinsky for television and was broadcast on June 14, 1962. There was singing, dialogue, and dance (choreographed by Mr. B). I was one of the sisters, which was not actually a dancing role, but Mr. B choreographed the movement of the whole piece, even entrances and exits. We wore long white dresses and very large constructed heads with exaggerated facial features that fit over our own heads. By most accounts, it was not successful, in this first rendition anyway. Regarding the choreography, Walter Terry described: "Choreographically, *Noah and the Flood* does not represent the most exciting and meaty of the Stravinsky-Balanchine collaborations but, during its brief course, it gives us a few special images of movement beauty which only Balanchine could devise."[14] Overall, the different elements were not that strong individually and did not mesh well.

But I would emphatically say that working with Mr. B while he was choreographing was always deeply inspiring, and my confidence grew with each new piece. Always prepared, he would come into the studio and start working right away. He would play the music at home (he was a talented musician), and when he came into the studio, he knew exactly what he wanted. He didn't agonize over steps like other choreographers often do. He didn't explain things in great detail: We generally knew what he wanted because we had all come up through SAB. Mr. B knew what made us look good and what we could do best. I don't mean that the work was not challenging, but, at least for the most part, it was not as if you had to work on it in the studio for three weeks and then still would not quite get it. Most of the time, his choreography was what we already did well. He knew what he wanted. His style was to demonstrate, and we would replicate his steps and impose our own individual style on top. We were "showing" the movement. "Be like Vogue model," he would say. His choreography was not meant to be internal but to be shown, presentational, and without fake smiles, although he did want us to smile sincerely in certain ballets. In general, Mr. B was not interested in the so-called soul of a dancer. What he wanted from us was complete, full-out, honest dancing, without pretense—no furrowing the brow, no suffering to portray emotion. Everything that needed to be conveyed in his choreography was built into the choreography as long as we danced full out and with all the energy we could muster. There was always more we could do in his eyes physically, though, like higher extensions, faster petit allegro.

He was also aware of and participated in every aspect concerning the production of his ballets. He attended to every detail, from costuming to the tempi of the orchestra. Mr. B was indeed a despot in that way, yet his was generally a gentle tyranny for he rarely lost his temper. He was always soft-spoken and never raised his voice. I can remember one incident related to my hairstyle. I had been wearing my hair in the traditional "classical" bun for *Swan Lake*, as I had been instructed to do by the other dancers. Mr. B came over to me before one performance and stared at my head for a long time. "Dear," he said, "your hair looks like bathing cap." I laughed, but after looking in the mirror I could see that "winging" the hair over the ears indeed looked as if I was wearing a bathing cap. From then on, we wore our hair pulled straight back and off our ears in what came to be known as the "Balanchine bun."

Even with Mr. B being hyperalert to all aspects of the company, including us as personnel, we never had weigh-ins or fines for infractions such as messy hair like some other companies. I remember in the grands battements in *The Four Temperaments* at one performance, one dancer's shoe flew off, which could have been a fineable offense, but I doubt she was fined.

One thing that did make him angry, however, was his dancers smoking marijuana or using cocaine, any illegal drug use. Balanchine had zero tolerance for it, and everyone knew that, so there was very little drug use in the company, although I was very naïve and might have been unaware of what was going on. I remember only three dancers who were fired, but there may have been more. By being so firm about the use of drugs, Mr. B kept the company much "cleaner" than some other dance companies.

The next big and very memorable event of my career was the European/Soviet Union tour in the fall of 1962, the first tour of New York City Ballet to the Soviet Union. We would be following on the success of American Ballet Theatre's tour there in 1960, but we would be presenting very different repertoire. This was also the first international tour for many of the company members, including me. Many of us were still in our teens. And it was Mr. B's first trip back since he left in 1924. A momentous occasion. There were sixty-one dancers, and we were accompanied by Mr.

B, Lincoln Kirstein, Betty Cage (general manager), our company doctor (Mel Kiddon), four conductors and pianists, a stage manager and small crew, wardrobe personnel (including the formidable Mme. Pourmel), and chaperones for underage dancers, plus, in the Soviet Union, several interpreters.[15] In addition, the American dance critic John Martin traveled with us, reporting back in the *New York Times*. We worked with the orchestras in the cities where we performed. The Bolshoi Ballet toured the United States and Canada while we toured the Soviet Union as a kind of artistic exchange. It was a huge State Department diplomatic affair.

But the tour almost did not happen. There were complicated negotiations.[16] In addition, NYCB management was worried about Mr. B being detained in the Soviet Union, and Mr. B was not thrilled about traveling to his homeland, which had been so drastically altered.[17] He considered himself very much American at that point—why go back? Mr. B had completely embraced the freedom and prosperity in the United States. Conditions in Russia were terrible when he left. They were practically starving, with little to no heat in a freezing-cold climate, and his life was very structured and proscribed there. Here in the United States, he choreographed for movies and Broadway, and he had all the food he could want. He had it in him to be able to adapt; he liked the freedom, which he found in the United States, to be able to create his own career however he wanted. One wonders if Lincoln Kirstein knew this about Mr. B when he helped him establish himself here in the United States. He certainly knew Mr. B had talent, but did he know or guess how Mr. B would embrace the United States and the American spirit of freedom and individuality? Mr. B famously said: "I am a potato. I can grow anywhere," but he truly loved the United States. With Mr. B seeming to have no desire to go back to the Soviet Union, the U.S. State Department pleaded to his sense of American patriotism—that this was an important mission to establish American dominance in an art form that had flowered in Russia.[18] It was really a kind of cultural warfare.[19]

My family was especially fearful about my going, because we were in the middle of the Cold War and I would be gone for three months. When the company was leaving, on August 29th, my parents and my cousin Barbara's family drove me to Idlewild airport (now John F. Kennedy airport). I left them, boarded the plane, and we were off! We began our tour with a landing in Amsterdam, The Netherlands.

One of the drawbacks of touring in any new city is that one sees mainly the inside of the theater and the hotel room. And when there is a day or an hour free, one is often too tired to take advantage of it. That was pretty much true of this tour, unfortunately. We performed in Hamburg, Berlin, Zurich, Stuttgart, Cologne, Frankfurt, and Vienna for a period of a month and then the Soviet Union for two months. The Western European part of the tour was very successful. The *New York Times* ran a short column titled "New York City Ballet Hailed by Newspapers of Vienna," which specifically stated that the newspaper *Die Presse* described the company as "the best dancing ensemble in the world" and George Balanchine as the "greatest choreographer."[20] The dancers were further praised in *Die Presse* as "unique personalities" who by "cooperating with the genius of the master . . . reach lonely peaks in this art."[21]

Despite our success in Western Europe, the Soviet Union was the most interesting and memorable part of the tour for me. We went to Moscow, Leningrad, Kiev, Tbilisi, and Baku. What a thrill to dance in the historic Bolshoi and Maryinsky theaters. One felt a sense of history while in these theaters that did not exist in the modern theaters where we also performed and that to me seemed architecturally cold. But it took time to get used to the raked stages in those grand old theaters. (Raked stages are tilted slightly toward the audience, hence the stage directions upstage and downstage.)

Our longest stay in one city was two weeks in Moscow, where we began the tour. I was constantly aware of the military there, with tanks rumbling down the street at weird hours, like during the night. We stayed in the Hotel Ukraine, which had an enormous lobby. I remember thinking that it looked like Grand Central Station! And the elevators were also huge, as if they were used to move herds of livestock. I have no idea why. There were floors where the elevators would not stop that we guessed might be used for surveillance. We were warned to be very careful of what we were saying in our rooms, as they would probably be bugged, and that even the waiters in the restaurant of the hotel might be reporting back to intelligence officials of the KGB (Soviet Union intelligence agency).[22] I also remember the tremendous pressure to perform at our very best. Mr. B told us in a company meeting before we left to take care in our appearances—no pants for the women, only nice dresses and skirts. We were representing not only the United States, but also New York City Ballet and Mr. B.

We performed at the Bolshoi, the first American dance company to do so, then moved to the much newer and much larger Palace of Congresses in the Kremlin, which seats 6,000 people, and later back to the Bolshoi.[23] Opening night at the Bolshoi Theater was October 9th. I remember they played the national anthems of both countries, and then we went right into *Serenade*. Other ballets performed on opening night were *Interplay* (by Jerome Robbins), *Agon*, and *Western Symphony*, in that order. The gravity of it all was fantastic. John Martin sent a review back to the *New York Times* noting that our program of short story-less ballets, including "three without scenery and costuming, is in marked contrast to the usual full evening of sumptuously produced ballets characteristic of the theater's regular procedure."[24] He also noted that response on the opening night was lukewarm at the beginning but delighted by the end.[25] It took time for the audience to warm to Balanchine's style, and then the final ballet, *Western Symphony*, was a kind of crowd pleaser with scenery and somewhat of a plot. ANTA (American National Theatre and Academy) and the State Department had selected ballets to be performed on this tour that reflected the company's neoclassical and abstract aesthetic but that were also accessible, and that did not contain any suggestion of violence (like Jerome Robbins's *The Cage*).[26] We were cultural ambassadors demonstrating the high quality and innovation of ballet in the United States.

Toward the end of our time in Moscow, Martin wrote of the performances: "Every one of the leading dancers has become no less than a favorite, and the excellence of the ensemble has been received with high favor.... [I]t is doubtful if even New York itself has ever seen the organization in such superb form or at such a high pitch."[27]

Throughout the tour, I understand, Soviet press response was guarded, but I remember that audience response generally ranged from enthusiastic to ecstatic.

One thing that left something to be desired in the older theaters was the plumbing. On arriving backstage the first day at the Bolshoi Theater, Mr. B wrinkled his nose and sniffed. "Smells like Monte Carlo," he said, referring to his own days as a dancer and choreographer touring with Diaghilev's Ballets Russes. We asked what he meant, and he replied, "pee-pee." Although there were toilets at the Palace of Congresses, at others, like the Bolshoi, we were not so lucky. Instead, we faced a room with a hole in the floor and two places on either side for our feet. With many of us suffering from bad diarrhea, which we named Moscow tummy, one can imagine the hole in the floor presented particular difficulties. We had also been warned to bring our own toilet paper if we didn't wish to use yesterday's newspaper. That toilet paper came in handy. In addition, I don't think the sun shone once the two weeks we were there in Moscow. The grayness was pervasive. And I felt the military presence more acutely in Moscow than the other cities. I remember we were having dinner one evening and could barely hear each other because of military tanks rumbling down the street like a parade, except that it was night. Most everyone felt depressed, and our arrival in Leningrad was a welcome change.

Leningrad was beautiful, and except for a few bedbugs in the hotel, our stay there was pleasant and inspiring. This was the city where Marius Petipa had choreographed some of his greatest ballets and where Balanchine and so many of our SAB teachers had trained. I watched class at the Vaganova School and was surprised at how they sprinkled water from a watering can on the floor to prevent slipping. There was something special about performing at the Maryinsky Theater because of its immense history. We performed there only two nights before moving to the theater in the Lensoviet Palace of Culture, which was much less opulent and held much less history.[28]

The performances were sold out and the audience response we could hear was strong, but because of limited interaction with the Soviet citizens, we did not have much personal feedback. We also did not have much interaction with the Kirov Ballet dancers or dancers in any of the cities we visited, but some of them attended performances. The following statements give a sense of a few individuals' responses. As reported in her biography, seeing Balanchine's abstract ballets, particularly *Apollo*, was a profound experience for Kirov ballerina Alla Osipenko: "Watching what was to a Russian very cool, abstract choreography, she was overcome with emotion."[29] Rachel Marcy wrote that Soviet citizen Lyudmilla Slutskaya saw the company perform on this tour and said it "felt like the rock and roll music being smuggled into the U.S.S.R."[30] John Martin reported that composer Aram Khatchaturian said: "The only shortcoming of the American ballet troupe is the absence of a story line. But this shortcoming is made up by the brilliant technique of the artists."[31] This last one amuses me because, of course, the absence of a story line was a key point of Balanchine's choreography—this is what the company was all about! Of course, Balanchine's innovations in ballet were so different from what they had seen and experienced up until then, and this tour was also during the Cold War. It is unlikely that any Soviet Union publication at the time would have given rave reviews because those would have been reserved for their own companies. Writing several decades later in 2011, Russian dance writer Elizabeth Souritz, who was in the audience of the 1962 NYCB performances in Moscow, described the importance of performances by foreign companies, including NYCB, on the development of the art form in the Soviet Union: "They opened new horizons to Soviet choreographers, dancers, and even audiences, liberalized the artistic effort of those working in the arts toward new forms of expression."[32]

We flew in a "prop" plane from Leningrad to Kiev. The stewardesses (not called flight attendants in those days) wore babushkas on their heads as part of their uniform, and the meal was ice-cold chicken with peas, only they had not finished thawing out the food and certainly didn't warm anything up. Yum.

I don't remember too much of Kiev except that the weather was cold and wet, and everyone seemed to be getting sick. The weather, in addition to limited food choices, was taking its toll. There was a lot of bread and potatoes and very few fresh green vegetables. We had been instructed to bring food and cleaning supplies with us (in addition to toilet paper), and I had done this. I don't remember the specifics, but Rachel Marcy states that we were allowed to bring a footlocker with up to 106 pounds of nonperishable foods, toilet paper, and cleaning supplies.[33] I do remember particularly bringing canned tuna and peanut butter, but I longed for something more akin to my regular diet. And, unfortunately, I had to put the cleaning supplies to good use. When we checked into the hotel in Kiev, there were feces behind the toilet on the floor. So there I was, on my hands and knees, cleaning the floor with my bleach cleanser—disgusting!

The city of Tbilisi is in the Georgian region, which is where Balanchine's family hailed from. We were treated to wonderful Georgian dancing at a party for Mr. B and his brother Andrei Balanchivadze, who was a composer. They hadn't seen each other in over forty years. At the party, we had little oranges for the first time since arriving in the Soviet Union and authentic shashlik, a kind of shish kebab. The food was tasty, which was rare on this tour. I also had the opportunity to see the famous Vakhtang Chabukiani (1910–1992) perform. I was so impressed by his wild energy and theatricality. His exaggerated facial expressions made his performance almost campy, but not quite. He came across as a true artist. I marveled that wherever we were in the Soviet Union, there always was a wonderful ballet company and an appreciative audience.

By the time we arrived in Baku, our final city, we were all so happy to be going home soon that our mood was jovial. It had been a long tour—a month in Europe followed by two months in the Soviet Union, and everyone was exhausted and eager to be home. Our last performance was on December 1st. Then we traveled back to Moscow. The day we left the Soviet Union, the airport in Moscow was about to be shut down because of heavy snow. Ours was the last plane allowed to take off, and hours later, we arrived in the Copenhagen airport for a short stopover. We went wild! We hadn't seen civilization as we knew it in so long we didn't know what to buy first. I bought a sweater, some cheese, and, of course, chocolate. Then we boarded a charter SAS flight and finished our journey. I am so glad that I was part of the tour, but I had no desire to go back to the Soviet Union ever. I left the company shortly before the next Soviet tour.

One of the aspects I found most wearing was that we were watched so closely by the Russians the whole time, which got exhausting after a while. Since I didn't know the Russian language or the alphabet, I was afraid to venture out on my own. I didn't feel free to walk around. I didn't want to involve myself in any situation that might have been potentially dangerous. We had been told we would be dismissed from the tour for

Serenade in Tbilisi, Soviet Union, 1962. I am on the right in foreground with Ellen Shire on the left. Photographer unknown.

misconduct, which was a kind of nebulous warning. I certainly didn't want to call attention to myself in any negative way, but I know I missed a lot. Some of the more adventurous company members saw much more. One adventure I did have was visiting Gum department store, in Moscow. It was strange because there was so little on the shelves, but I did

New York City Ballet - November 1962 - Baku

NYCB in Baku, Soviet Union, 1962. I am fourth from the right, seated on the front row with my legs in front of me. Some of the other people in the photo are—*Front row seated from left*: Edward Bigelow, Patricia McBride, John Taras, Jillana, William Weslow. *Middle row kneeling*: Arthur Mitchell (in striped t-shirt). *First row standing*: Balanchine (partial view on far left), Diana Adams (in plaid robe), Sara Leland (in sweater), Earle Sieveling, Janet Villella, Edward Villella, Melissa Hayden (seventh, sixth, fifth, fourth from right). *Standing toward back*: Jacques d'Amboise (in open-collar dark shirt), John Martin (behind d'Amboise with arms crossed), Robert Irving (in light jacket and tie, behind Diana Adams), Nicholas Magallanes (waving). Photographer unknown.

buy a little black enamel painted box, which I still have. And I visited Vladimir Lenin's Mausoleum in Moscow with a group of fellow dancers. Lenin's body was preserved when he died in 1924 and placed under glass for public viewing. There was something about it that was very macabre, and we got a bit silly, referring to his body as "the cold cut."

The Cuban Missile Crisis happened while we were in the Soviet Union at the beginning of the tour, but I was only vaguely aware. I don't remember being given much information until after the crisis was over. While we were there, I figured if there were an imminent crisis, they would send us home, but it clearly would not have been as simple as that. Lincoln Kirstein apparently presented an emergency plan for us to leave the Soviet Union to the United States embassy officials, and they said, "*You* don't have plans. You leave when they tell you to leave."[34] It was very scary to hear about the Cuban Missile Crisis when we got back to the United States; only then did I realize the full danger we had all faced. Two years ago, I was contacted by the BBC radio station in New York to give my thoughts on the Cuban Missile Crisis while we were in the Soviet Union in 1962. I explained that I had not known much of what was going on while we were in the Soviet Union. Allegra Kent also gave an interview, which was very different from mine. She understood much more of what was happening with the Cuban Missile Crisis than I did while we were on the tour. She was evidently terrified and desperately wanted to go home. She said if she was going to die, she wanted to be with her children. The seriousness of the situation only became real to me much later as I realized how close we had come to nuclear war.

It was during that European/Soviet Union tour that I had my first inkling of Balanchine's attitude about weight. I had always been a painfully thin child and could always eat whatever I wanted without ever gaining weight. Unfortunately, I was no longer a child, and my overindulgence in Viennese pastry, schlag (whipped cream), and enormous omelets with fine herbs for breakfast was beginning to show. "Mr. B suggests that you lose some weight," I was told by Diana Adams. "Your weight should be 116 pounds, certainly no more than 120." I was really upset, and I started dieting that very day. I found, however, that dieting in Europe was rather difficult, and although I was careful not to eat pastry and bread, I decided to wait until we returned to the States before dieting in earnest.

I dieted religiously all through the winter season and, by the end, had shed at least nine pounds. I ate mostly protein, chopped steak, eggs, yogurt, fruits and vegetables, bran muffins—no pasta, no white bread, no liquor, no dessert, and the weight came off. I knew Mr. B had noticed my weight loss and that made me doubly proud. Unfortunately, I gained some of the weight back on the layoff, and, by the start of the next season's rehearsal period, I was again "too heavy." Unknowingly, I had established a pattern of behavior that was to plague me all my years in the company.

In the beginning, my being "overweight" didn't seem to be much of a problem. In fact, Mr. B often joked about it. I remember one day I was on the eighth floor of City Center, and I happened to pass Mr. B's office. He called me in and after exchanging the usual "how are you's?" he took my hand and started squeezing my fingers. When I asked what he was doing, he reminded me of the story of Hansel and Gretel. Did I remember the old witch who in order to tell whether the children were plump enough for eating, would squeeze their fingers every day? Of course, we both laughed. I guess I could never really believe that five or six pounds could make a difference to Mr. B when he seemed to like my dancing so much. After all, I was dancing a lot and starting to do little demi-solos as well. This isn't to say that I stopped dieting. I was always dieting, but somehow I would finish a season thin and start the next season heavy again.

I remember one company class where he came and stood in front of me and kind of patted me all over and said, "You look pregnant, dear." And it was awful, really awful to hear him say that. I can't remember if it was in front of the whole class, but it was embarrassing. Another time he said, "You are like inside a cocoon; your true personality will only be revealed when all the fat is gone, and you are down to your bones. Now maybe you will do it." And, of course, like all the times before and all the times to come, I decided this would be the season I would be thin and stay thin.

Thinness was very important to Mr. B in his dancers, and I think he was right to an extent. He didn't want us to be anorexic; he didn't want us to starve ourselves. He wanted thin dancers, not emaciated ones. At the weight I felt I looked best, and that Mr. B approved of, I still looked healthy, never emaciated. But his choreography, and I think all ballet choreography—whether it is his or someone else's—looks better on a trim body. The body needs to be the vehicle that illustrates the choreography to the fullest. If you have a little excess fat on you, your body isn't going to be able to show the choreography the way it needs to be shown. The muscles should show clearly so the lines are better.

There is so much negativity out there still about Mr. B and this concept of being super-thin, maybe below one's normal weight. But that "normal weight" is established for the general public. People sometimes have the mistaken idea that, for his dancers to look the way he wanted them to look, they had to be anorexic, and that he contributed to so many dancers today having eating disorders. Eating disorders did plague that era, and there were a few dancers in the company who were anorexic. However, while it is true that Mr. B would often reward you with roles if you lost weight, he surely didn't want us to be sick and unhealthy. Today, there is more of a focus on dancers' health and well-being. We understand better the ramifications of anorexia, bulimia, and starvation. The management of NYCB is necessarily having more input into awareness of healthy eating habits today. But Mr. B sort of left us alone to figure out how to lose weight, and if we did it, great! And if we didn't do it, we didn't get the roles. Or we might even be taken out of ballets.

When a dancer felt that Mr. B had confidence in her, then there was nothing she couldn't do. We would rise to his high level of expectation and improve. But the reverse was also true. By Mr. B ignoring a dancer, by expressing disapproval in some way, be it silently or with casting, a dancer could lose confidence in herself to the point where she would become paralyzed—afraid to try because she felt she couldn't possibly win his approval. It took an extremely strong-willed dancer to say, "I don't care if he approves or not, I'm dancing for myself." For me, Mr. B became the "daddy" whom that little girl wanted to please. Unfortunately, although I knew what I had to do, I was unable to do it—consistently keep the extra pounds off. Although my career appeared to be moving forward, I was really holding myself back.

In retrospect, it seems odd. Here I was, a good dancer, good enough to make the best company in the United States. My career was clearly going well. Balanchine liked me and cared enough to give me significant roles. And, yet, I would go home some nights after performance and eat a can of nuts or a whole Sara Lee cake. Then, I could barely face him the next day in class, consumed with guilt and sure that I had gained five pounds overnight. I had become a binge eater, but I never threw up—I couldn't stand the thought. After a performance, I would be in my apartment, and, at 1:00 in the morning, I would put a raincoat on over my pajamas and go downstairs to a convenience store/deli on Amsterdam Avenue called Smiler's. I would buy a loaf of ordinary white bread and eat the whole loaf with butter and jam, and I don't even like to eat bread. Craziness! I guess I felt I was under so much extreme pressure to be thin. Clearly, I had an eating disorder. My refusal to get on a scale was another example of my inability to "do something about myself." I insisted I wanted to be thin, but my actions spoke louder than my words. I even went to a psychiatrist to find out why I could not lose weight and keep it off. Through therapy, I found I was really conflicted about my career and success, success that might prevent me from getting married and having a child, which were both very much part of my plans, hopes, and dreams. I found myself lacking motivation sometimes as much as I loved to dance. I often wonder whether my inability to keep my weight down was a form of rebellion. I was always such a good girl. I never

Gounod Symphony, 1963. Carol Sumner (*right*) and I (*left*) are on pointe. Photo by Martha Swope ©Billy Rose Theatre Division, The New York Public Library for the Performing Arts.

smoked, never did drugs, always tried to be perfect. Maybe I needed to rebel in some way.

On January 18, 1963, New York City Ballet performed excerpts from Balanchine's *Stars and Stripes* for "The Inaugural Anniversary Salute for President John F. Kennedy." Principal dancers Allegra Kent, Edward Villella, and Arthur Mitchell performed along with the corps of men and women. It was an honor to be part of a glittering night of stars from opera, motion pictures, the Broadway stage, folk music, and dance as we paid tribute to the president. Mrs. Kennedy may well have had a hand in planning the performance aspect of the event as she particularly valued and supported the arts. She used to attend performances of *The Nutcracker* at the State Theater with her daughter Caroline. They would come backstage, and Mrs. Kennedy would speak in French with Mr. B.

When President Kennedy was assassinated less than a year later on November 22, 1963, I was on the Broadway bus heading to City Center for rehearsal. People on the bus were crying. It seemed so unbelievable that something like that could happen in this country. Assassination was something that happened far back in history—not in modern times. And yet, it had happened and would happen again. We did rehearse that day, but in silence.

Chapter 4

New York City Ballet, Soloist

New York City Ballet moved to the New York State Theater (now the David H. Koch Theater) in Lincoln Center in 1964, which was a landmark event for the company. It was a brand-new state-of-the-art theater, with a stage much larger than City Center, which had been our home. The State Theater was designed by Philip Johnson, but with Mr. B's input.[1] Although I know now that there was much controversy surrounding the theater and NYCB's residence there,[2] at the time I was unaware and just excited to be moving to this beautiful new space. We opened there on April 23rd, performing *Allegro Brillante* and *Stars and Stripes*.[3] I have vivid memories of taking company class at the State Theater. Each company member had her or his own special spot at the barre.

In 1964, we also signed our first full-year contracts,[4] and I was made a soloist. This happened just as we were moving to the New York State Theater. I was so proud. I was no longer to dress way upstairs in the big corps dressing room. I now shared a dressing room with other soloists (Carol Sumner, Gloria Govrin, and Teena McConnell) on the second floor. Teena and I were made soloists at the same time. We each had our own table and mirror plus a private bathroom and, the best part, our names on the door. As a soloist, sometimes your costumes would even be brought up to your dressing room.

After being made a soloist, I wanted to thank Mr. B as soon as I could, so I approached him after class one morning. I kissed him and said thank you, not knowing what else to say and waited for him to speak. "You don't have to thank me, dear," he said. "I'm running a business here—I do what I have to do for the public. Besides, I made you soloist in the hope that maybe now you might do something about yourself." He didn't deflate me entirely, but some of my elation was gone. I know that

In costume for *La Valse*, backstage at the New York State Theater, circa 1964. Photographer unknown.

he wouldn't have made me a soloist if my dancing weren't good enough, so I realized that my dancing was not the issue. It was my weight.

As exciting as it was to be named a soloist, I would have to say that I think my technical ability dropped a bit. In the corps, I danced in several ballets a night, sometimes four. It was exhausting, but I was in fantastic shape. Oddly enough, after being made a soloist I seemed to have less and less to dance. On some level it was nice not to have four ballets a night, but dancing that much had kept me in shape. What became difficult was keeping myself at that level of performance without the performances. And, of course, the less I danced, the more nervous I became when I had to dance. My solos made me very nervous. Mr. B always watched from the wings, and all I could think was, "he's staring at my thighs." I felt that all my flaws were magnified tenfold and wished he would go out front.

In 1964, I was cast as a demi-soloist in Balanchine's new ballet, *Clarinade*, the first of his ballets to be staged at the New York State Theater.[5]

In rehearsal for *Clarinade*, 1964. *From left to right*: Richard Rapp, me, Mr. B, Suzanne Farrell, Anthony Blum. Photo by Martha Swope ©Billy Rose Theatre Division, The New York Public Library for the Performing Arts.

This was also one of the first ballets in which I had a featured role, plus it contained one of Suzanne Farrell's first leading roles. My partner was Robert Rodham, and we shared the stage with Carol Sumner, Richard Rapp, Suzanne, Anthony Blum, Arthur Mitchell, and Gloria Govrin. Everything I was given to dance fit with my ability and personality. The partnering was interesting and challenging, and, on opening night, Benny Goodman performed the music. Mr. B seemed to be enamored of ponytails, so that was how we wore our hair. My long hair often got stuck on my lipstick when I whipped my head around. Ultimately, the ballet was poorly received so was dropped from repertory.

Allen Hughes of the *New York Times*, wrote of *Clarinade* that it "seems to have irritated many observers, and it has been dismissed as an embarrassing, unfunny joke by a number of them."[6] But he advised that "if you can manage, you will find much to think about and possibly to admire in the work."[7] Hardly a resounding endorsement. But this was an important ballet for my career because being cast in demi-soloist roles indicated Mr. B's positive interest in me.

One of the other roles I was given when made a soloist was the lead in the First Movement of *Western Symphony*. My partner was Michael Steele. It was a difficult dance with intricate partnering, and we were responsible for rehearsing the section on our own. I do not remember having been coached by anyone. Also, I was not at my thinnest, and although the women wore black tights, which were flattering, I really was not looking my best. At the end of the dance there was a shoulder sit in which I would jump up, and Michael would lift me onto his shoulder. I started mentally blocking on the lift, and, instead of keeping my body upright, I would lean forward, which made it impossible for Michael to complete the lift. Instead, never reaching his shoulder, I was sort of hanging up against his chest, and he was struggling to hold me there. What should have been a fun role turned into something I began to dread. Finally Mr. B took me out of it, and he was angry. He said probably the most hurtful thing he could have said to me: that people in the audience were wondering why I was dancing a principal role and was it because I was his girlfriend. I had just really let the pressure get to me in all my self-consciousness.

I have realized as I have gotten older that I was also sometimes afraid to try things in class, afraid of failing, of not being up to the high technical level I once had reached. Sometimes, if a combination (like turns) was given that I didn't feel confident about, I would hang out at the back of the room and not do it. That happened more when I was a soloist. I should have been shining at the top of the class, but I became more and more self-conscious. Also, I guess I kind of focused on what I did well, and I stopped working on the things I was not as good at, but that I should have been trying to perfect. A lot of dancing is mental, and I got myself into a negative mental place. Perhaps if I had been given more challenging roles, it would have forced me to keep my technique up and push myself more.

But there were definitely more positives than negatives about being made a soloist, including a significant bump in my salary. This allowed me to move out of my parents' apartment into a lovely little studio apartment near Lincoln Center ($265 per month rent). My parents stayed together, but they never got along very well, so it was wonderful to be on my own. I couldn't take the constant bickering anymore, and I needed independence.

With this newfound freedom, I began my first serious relationship with a violinist from the New York City Ballet Orchestra, whom I will call Jake (not his real name). I was twenty-three and he was twenty-five, and I fell head over heels in love with him. We would go on tour together because the orchestra generally traveled with the dancers. I would sneak around to his hotel room at night, and then back down or up the stairs to my room. Back in New York, we would sometimes spend all day together when we had a full day off. As a soloist, I also had some evenings off, and we would go to dinner. I began enjoying what I saw as a "real life," and it seemed that the less I did dance-wise, the less I wanted to do. Still, when I was at the theater, involved with rehearsals, casting, performing, I wanted that very much. I often wished that there were no layoffs so I could keep my feelings about the company straight, for it was always when I was away from the company, even for a day, that I found my motivation waning.

The years seemed to go by pretty much the same way with the company. Each season I would have at least one new role to learn, and I was dancing well. I went to class every morning, rehearsed all day, performed at night. Interestingly, Mr. B often asked other choreographers to set or create works on us. I think it was a way to take some pressure off himself to continually provide new choreography for the company.

When I first joined the company, and we were still performing at City Center, Lew Christensen's *Con Amore* was in the repertoire. I was cast as an Amazon soldier, and we danced with wooden rifles standing guard over the Camp against the marauding Bandit. Gloria Govrin was the lead Amazon and Edward Villella was the Bandit. The choreography was challenging without being too difficult, and the Gioachino Rossini music was exciting. I had the pleasure of rehearsing the ballet when my Purchase students performed it in the 1990s.

Antony Tudor choreographed or revived several ballets for the company in the late 1940s and early 1950s, and he then staged a revival of *Dim Lustre*, in 1964. First performed in 1943, *Dim Lustre* has more emotional content than most of Mr. B's work, so it was quite different for us. It is really about the poignancy of remembering and begins with dancers sweeping around the stage at a nineteenth-century ball. *Dim Lustre* was kept in the repertory for several years, and I was originally an understudy, but I did get to perform it. It was awkward choreography for me compared to Mr. B's. Mr. B's choreography just made sense physically and mathematically, but with Tudor's choreography, we were constantly changing directions in the middle of steps. He also had an acid tongue. He could be mean to the dancers. He was very sarcastic and seemed to take pleasure in being hurtful although he did not direct any of this specifically at me. There is a great story my friend (and former NYCB dancer) Lynne Stetson tells that Mr. Tudor was looking to see which dancer he would give a particular part to, and he asked how many glasses of champagne they could drink.[8] My friend Lynne said "Five," and she got the part![9] Another time, he was giving a step to the first cast, and they weren't all doing it right, so he turned to the understudies, which Lynne was. He asked them each to get up and try. New to the company, Lynne had not been watching that carefully, so she got up and just faked a few steps.[10] He was silent for the longest time looking at her, and then he said, "You little faker!"[11] I don't know if I would have had the guts to do that! Nothing got past him. But he had a sense of humor.

I also learned and performed *Sarabande and Danse*, in 1970, with choreography by John Clifford and music by Claude Debussy. John was a dancer with NYCB from 1966 to 1974 and then guest artist from 1974 to 1980. I came to respect him enormously. He was an upstart, but Mr. B nurtured him and saw his talent and potential. He choreographed eight ballets for New York City Ballet, and he was widely considered to be Mr. B's protégé. He was young, too, to be given so much responsibility. Mr. B really tried to help him, even with establishing his ballet company in Los Angeles.

I learned three ballets by Jacques d'Amboise: *The Chase or The Vixen's Choice* (1963), *Irish Fantasy* (1964), and *Prologue* (1967), which was based on Shakespeare's *Othello*. (I was Mimi Paul's understudy in *Prologue*, and I don't remember if I performed it.) I thought Jacques was a very good choreographer. Working on his ballets was always a pleasant experience. He had a clear understanding of composition and structure and communicated that well.

Jacques joined NYCB when he was fifteen, so he really knew the inner workings of the company, and Mr. B was very close to him. I always felt that he understood what Balanchine wanted in class and choreographically. I admired his dancing completely. When Jacques had to make an entrance on stage he often would need a running start. He would go close to a wall in the back wing, push off that wall and come bursting on to the stage like an explosion! It was all about the energy; that was what Mr. B wanted and Jacques delivered. I was very pleased that Mr. B offered Jacques the opportunity to choreograph.

John Taras also choreographed a number of ballets at NYCB. I danced in two: *Piège de Lumière* (1952) and *Shadow'd Ground* (1965). When I joined the company, Maria Tallchief was still dancing, although she was nearing the time she would eventually retire. I had seen her perform when she was in her prime in ballets like *Firebird* and *Sylvia: Pas de Deux,* in which she showed her regal bearing and wonderful technique. In Taras's *Piège de Lumière*, she was the lead Butterfly, and Anthony Blum was her partner. Taras had devised an extremely awkward, but unusually beautiful lift. Tony would kneel with a flat back, and Maria would jump onto Tony's back and assume a birdlike pose. I was one of a group of butterflies in *Piège,* and there was a moment when we were traveling on the diagonal from downstage right to upstage left going into a strong stream of light, which completely blinded us as we flapped our arms and did a very complicated step. It was memorably difficult.

On January 20, 1965, NYCB once again performed at a presidential event, President Lyndon B. Johnson's Second Inauguration. We performed excerpts from *Western Symphony* probably chosen to honor the president's Texas origins. Folk singer Joan Baez also performed, singing while barefoot with her legs hanging down over the edge of the stage.

From June to September of the same year, NYCB toured Europe and the Middle East. We went to Paris, Milan, Spoleto, Venice, Dubrovnik,

Athens, Jerusalem, Tel Aviv, Salzburg, Amsterdam, and London. The ballet orchestra did not travel with us, so Jake was not along. My mother accompanied me on the tour. She did some traveling with Patricia Mc-Bride's mother, separate from the ballet company, but she was with us for part of the tour, too. Our time for sightseeing was extremely limited, maybe one day in each city. We mostly saw the inside of our hotel rooms and the theater.

Paris was so beautiful and romantic with such great food! And I loved Venice. I vowed to return one day as a tourist. In Milan, I remember the gorgeous and historic Galleria Vittorio Emanuele II, the four-storied covered shopping arcade, and that we stayed at the Hotel Marino alla Scala. We danced in Athens at the Odeon of Herodes Atticus, an amphitheater originally built in 161 A.D. *Serenade* outdoors, the opening pose looking up at the Parthenon all lit up, with that glorious Tchaikovsky music—it was a special moment indeed.

We were only in Jerusalem for one day, but I did walk the cobblestones of Jaffa Road. In Tel Aviv, our accommodations were outside of the city on a kibbutz called the Kfar Maccabiah. Breakfast at the Kfar consisted of a buffet, and all I can remember were the hard-boiled eggs with flies buzzing around them. That was it for most of us. We moved out and found hotels in the city. Most of the dancers wound up at the Dan Hotel, a beautiful place on the beach. I managed to find an Orthodox Jewish hotel called the Devorah, which did not use up as much of my per diem. Because the Devorah was Orthodox, on Saturdays (the Sabbath) buttons in the elevator were not allowed to be pressed because one is not supposed to work on the Sabbath, which includes pressing buttons. The elevator was set up so that it stopped on every floor. It took forever to get down to the street level and up to my room.

Mr. B choreographed *Harlequinade* in 1965, and I was in the premiere cast. Mr. B had danced in Petipa's version as a child in St. Petersburg,[12] and the music is by Riccardo Drigo, whom critic Walter Terry notes Balanchine had known in St. Petersburg.[13] So it seems that Balanchine was honoring and exploring parts of his childhood memories. *Harlequinade* is a delightful ballet and very enjoyable to dance. Often, Balanchine ballets have a central principal couple and then two or four demi-solo girls

Balanchine and me rehearsing *Harlequinade*, 1965. Photo by Martha Swope ©Billy Rose Theatre Division, The New York Public Library for the Performing Arts.

in featured roles. In *Harlequinade* there are four Scaramouche couples, friends of Harlequin and Columbine, but only the girls do any real dancing. The boys mainly partner. I was fortunate to have been one of those four demi-solo girls.

Rehearsals for our little dances were fun. My partner, Earle Sieveling, often made me laugh, but we were never distracted from Mr. B's process. The atmosphere in these rehearsals was always congenial yet serious. The photograph on the cover of this book as well as the one included in the sixth chapter were taken by Martha Swope during one of these rehearsals. Mr. B was trying to show the boys how to profess their love for us, and we ladies were always to be demure and reticent. The dance for the four girls allowed us to show our musicality and fast footwork.

Mr. B also choreographed *Don Quixote* in 1965, and again I was in the premiere cast. Although Richard Rapp and Francisco Moncion generally performed the lead role, I think Mr. B choreographed this ballet to show his profound love for Suzanne Farrell. He saw himself in the Don Quixote role and even performed it a few times. Suzanne was Dulcinea. One could feel slightly uncomfortable observing the connection between them when they danced together, almost as though watching them was an intrusion into their special relationship. I especially remember the image of Suzanne as Dulcinea washing the Don's feet and drying them with her hair. There was such poignancy and love depicted in that gesture. Edwin Denby wrote of the ballet: "Rich and strange, bitter, delicate, and tragic, the piece gathers in one's imagination. When it is finished, it seems to have become a somber story of alienation."[14]

My memories of performing this ballet are more vivid then the rehearsal process itself. I was cast at first in the "Jota," a folk dance among the townspeople in Act 1. John Taras, then ballet master, was assigned that piece of choreography. Typical of John's choreography, that section had very fast footwork and a step for every musical note. I was also cast as a courtier in the Ballroom scene. Wearing those long brown velvet dresses made us all feel elegant. Eventually I was cast as the Duchess, originally performed by Jillana, who mocks and toys with the Don. I really enjoyed that role as it was an opportunity for me to use my acting ability, and I was very comfortable with that. And then there was the funeral procession complete with incense and hooded monks. The ballet didn't survive very long in the repertoire, but there were some extraordinarily stunning moments of breathtaking dancing by Suzanne and Marnee Morris in the Dream sequence.

One of the major highlights of my career was being given the opportunity to perform one of the five ballerinas in the revised and expanded *Divertimento No. 15* in its premiere on April 27, 1966. (I had also danced in the corps de ballet of the 1956 version of the ballet.) Mr. B's impetus was always the music; however, he may have chosen Mozart's *Divertimento No. 15* because he wanted to do a ballet for five of his favorite ballerinas and three of his male soloists who were good partners. The music fit his plan—five variations for women and a sixth for the two soloist men, a minuet for the corps, five pas de deux, and an opening and finale for the entire cast.

I was not originally cast in the new version of the ballet, but I remem-

Divertimento No. 15, circa 1966. Richard Rapp and me. Photo by Fred Fehl. Photo courtesy Gabriel Pinski.

ber standing backstage getting ready to go on stage in *Agon*. I had been dieting, and it had paid off. I really looked good. I was in the wings, and Mr. B was also in the wings talking to Lincoln Kirstein. Carol Sumner had injured herself, and they were discussing who should replace her as one of the five principal women in *Divertimento No. 15*. I heard Mr. B say to Lincoln, "How about BJ?" I wasn't supposed to hear, but I did, and I could hardly contain myself. I was called to rehearsal the follow-ing day, and I learned the part in two days. For the new version, Mr. B was adding a cadenza in the finale, and I remember we rehearsed that section a lot. It was such an incredible honor to dance this role because I was still a soloist, and this was a principal's part generally. To be able to dance to that exquisite music on the great stage of the New York State Theater with that choreography—I mean what could be better? It was the most fulfilling aspect of being in the company. Clive Barnes gave a glowing review of the new production of *Divertimento No. 15*, praising the choreography and the dancers: "The company—each and every one of then—danced it deliciously."[15]

When I first performed the role, Mr. B had been out front in the audience, but he came backstage to tell me, "Very good, dear." Coming from him, that was a huge compliment! He didn't say it often or to many people. I knew that although I was technically capable of dancing the role, one of the reasons I was cast was that I was at my very thinnest. Mr. B often "rewarded" his dancers when they did something for him, and my getting thin was for him. Of course, it should have been for me, but it wasn't, at least not entirely. This is only the beginning, I thought. More and more roles will follow. Although they didn't just then, I was encouraged. I knew Mr. B thought highly of me, and I felt confident just knowing he thought me capable of principal roles. I remember performing the ballet that season but, as usual, I started gaining the weight back, and I was not designated to perform *Divertimento No. 15* in the next season. I had never asked Mr. B for anything, but I asked him to please let me dance *Divert* again. He reluctantly agreed, and I was cast, but it was not the same. I knew I didn't have his support or approval. I never danced that part again.

In May of 1966, just a few days after the premiere of *Divertimento No. 15*, I received a nice mention from Clive Barnes in the *New York Times* about my performance in *Swan Lake*: "and I particularly liked the freshness of Bettijane Sills in the Pas de Neuf."[16] I had been dancing *Swan Lake* since I entered the company. It was one of my first roles, although I had not always danced the Pas de Neuf. It was a surprise to be mentioned in the press out of the blue, but very pleasing.

In July of 1966, we traveled to Saratoga Springs in upstate New York, where NYCB first performed at the new Saratoga Performing Arts Center. The opening night ballet was *A Midsummer Night's Dream*. Saratoga became the permanent summer home for the company for the month of July. While we were in residence there as a company, we generally found our own accommodations. Some people rented houses or stayed in town at the Rip Van Dam or the Adelphi. I usually stayed at the elegant Gideon Putnam Hotel located in the Saratoga Spa State Park, and it was a lovely place to stay. (I still stay there every time I visit.) Once I roomed with Suki Schorer, but usually I roomed alone. We could walk to the theater and to the Victoria Pool, which was also in the Saratoga Spa State Park. The hotel opened the dining room early, at 5 p.m., so we could have dinner before the performance. In those days, I ate a full dinner before a performance. Later, I changed and didn't eat dinner before dancing. Performing on an empty stomach was more comfortable.

I once ran into Mr. B and Hubert Saal (longtime music and dance critic for *Newsweek*) having lunch outdoors at the Gideon Putnam Hotel. I sat with them, and all they did was gossip about the company members. Who was sleeping with whom? It was amusing, I must say. Mr. B loved a juicy piece of gossip. A few times, I stayed in town at the Rip Van Dam Hotel, which had a swimming pool right in the middle of the parking lot. The rooms were kind of grubby and inelegant, but it was nice being in town. I didn't drive, so I would either take the bus into the park or bum rides from the other company members who had rented cars. I went every year to Saratoga and loved it. Even though we were working, it was like a vacation. In the summer of 2016, New York City Ballet celebrated its 50th anniversary of being in residence in Saratoga. Very appropriately, they performed *A Midsummer Night's Dream*. I was at the performance, and it was wonderful.

In the fall of 1966, we toured to Montreal where we performed for a week at the Salle Wilfrid-Pelletier at Place des Arts.[17] There is a film of *Concerto Barocco* from then, and I am in it. We also performed in Toronto.

In 1967, I was in the original cast of the "Diamonds" section of *Jewels*, one of the four demi-soloists, a huge opportunity. This ballet stands as one of Mr. B's finest, and I am honored to have been part of the creation. Mr. B worked with that familiar configuration of the principal couple with four featured couples and then the corps. Carol Sumner and I shared featured sections in the opening Waltz. With the remaining two demi-soloist girls, we returned in the Scherzo, which was interspersed with variations for Jacques d'Amboise and Suzanne Farrell. The final movement was an exciting Polonaise for the entire cast.

Robert Garis described the ballet in *Partisan Review*:

> *Jewels* is Balanchine's gift not only to us but to this great company. It is unquestionably a major work, and most of it is in the absolutely top class of *Apollo*, *The Four Temperaments*, *Agon*, *Episodes*, *Liebeslieder Walzer*. But I admire *Jewels* because it is a big hit and was meant to be: I like being reminded again of the supreme theatrical instinct that links Balanchine with Shakespeare and Mozart as the kind of genius who can obey and even enjoy and want the necessity of pleasing an audience.[18]

The ballet has three distinct sections: "Emeralds," "Rubies," and "Diamonds" with very different music for each, and therefore very different corresponding choreography. "Emeralds" is lyrical, "Rubies" is jazzy, and "Diamonds" is classical and austere. Mr. B is said to have been inspired by a visit to the jewelers Van Cleef and Arpels. "Emeralds" and "Rubies" were wonderful pieces of choreography danced by great artists, but I always felt that "Diamonds" was special to Mr. B because it was done for his love, Suzanne Farrell.

We toured to Montreal again in July 1967, for Expo '67, and danced *Jewels* among other works, once again performing at the Salle Wilfrid-Pelletier at Place des Arts.[19] From there, we went to Saratoga Springs for our regular season. Part of the company (twenty-five dancers) then went to the Edinburgh Festival in Scotland for a week at the end of August. Where we performed in Edinburgh was usually used as a bingo hall, and a rehearsal had to be stopped one day for a bingo game. Mr. B gave his thoughts on this: "'Of course bingo is more important than ballet,' he said. 'It makes money.'"[20] I remember being at my absolute thinnest in Scotland and that Mr. B was really watching me. But then we came home to a layoff, and I gained much of the weight back again. Such self-sabotage. This layoff was particularly difficult for other reasons, too.

My boyfriend Jake had left the ballet orchestra in 1966 and joined another musical group, and I would travel with them sometimes. It was a wonderful time for him—a fantastic position to have. I would travel in the car with the group when they were going somewhere nearby. And there would be parties for his group, and I attended when I could. But somehow, we began to drift apart. I don't think his parents ever liked me very well, maybe because I was Jewish, and they were not, and that probably contributed to the distance that was forming between Jake and me. We began to settle into a kind of friendship more than a romance. I began to feel both hurt and neglected, although we did not really discuss it.

So I got involved with someone else, another musician, while I was in Edinburgh with NYCB. When I returned home, I wrote Jake a "Dear John" letter, which I regret to this day. He got very angry, and it was really the end of our relationship. Even though I precipitated it, I was devastated. My mother was very upset with me because she and my father adored Jake. He was a sweet, talented young man.

Afterward, I got involved with a married man who was also a musician who played in the ballet orchestra. Getting involved with a married man was a tremendous mistake. He said he was going to leave his wife. We were going to buy an apartment together. That didn't happen. My mother really disliked him, and after a while I realized I had made a mistake. So that relationship ended, too, but it was more a feeling of "good riddance" than the despair I felt over Jake.

All the while, our society was moving through the turbulent and violent 1960s. On April 4, 1968, Dr. Martin Luther King Jr. was assassinated. The event rocked the nation, and Mr. B immediately began choreographing *Requiem Canticles*, which was a tribute to Dr. King. It premiered on May 2, 1968, and was only performed once. I am honored to have danced in it. Clive Barnes described it as: "A ritual in homage to Dr. King set to Stravinsky's 1966 score, this could never be a repertory piece, and is not intended as such, but as an act of homage to a fallen leader, it had dignity and grandeur."[21] I remember that the rehearsals were a bit tedious, mostly because there was not much dancing involved. We stood around a lot in a big semicircle, and we did a lot of walking, carrying candelabras. Arthur Mitchell was the central figure. We, as dancers in the company, were very aware of the seriousness and were respectful of Mr. B's process.

A highlight of 1969 was traveling to Monte Carlo to take part in the

Diaghilev Festival, which celebrated the sixtieth anniversary of the founding of Diaghilev's Ballets Russes. The festival took place in June, and we stayed at the Hotel Hermitage. I was impressed by the elegance and wealth. There were all the yachts, so different from the lifestyle I knew. At a special dinner, given by Princess Grace and Prince Rainier for the principal dancers, our manager apparently drank too much and fell into his soup. He was sitting next to British actor David Niven, who reportedly said, "Is that all he does?" I was not there, but the story was all the "talk" throughout the tour.

In 1969, Suzanne Farrell married Paul Mejia, and it had a major effect on the whole company. In her autobiography, *Holding On to the Air*, Suzanne talks about her unique and complex relationship with Mr. B and her not wanting to lose that, but also not wanting to marry him.[22] Suzanne's hasty marriage to fellow dancer Paul Mejia, just as Mr. B was divorcing his wife Tanaquil Le Clercq to be free to marry Suzanne, was probably Suzanne's way of preventing a possible future she found intolerable. And she loved Paul.

But none of this was known to me at that time. In fact, I thought Suzanne wanted to marry Mr. B and was quite content with their relationship. I often saw Suzanne, Paul, and at times, Suzanne's friend, Gail Crisa, leaving the theater after a performance to go to dinner with Mr. B. I thought nothing of Paul's presence since Mr. B had a special fondness for him. The fact that Suzanne and Paul were having a serious relationship came as a complete surprise to me and, of course, to Mr. B. When they married, he fell apart.

As I remember, shortly after Suzanne and Paul married, the whole situation came to a head with Mr. B taking Paul out of the third movement of *Symphony in C*, and then Suzanne demanded he put Paul back in or they would both resign. He didn't, and Suzanne and Paul left the company. Mr. B had encouraged Paul to choreograph on the company, and there were only a handful of dancers who did. Like Mr. B, Paul also played the piano. Mr. B saw himself as Paul's mentor, and then Paul married the woman for whom Mr. B had divorced Tanny (Tanaquil Le Clercq). Mr. B couldn't handle it. He fled to Europe in despair, meaning not to come back. The company was rudderless. No new ballets, no Mr. B standing in his customary spot in the downstage right wing watching us. Eventually, Barbara Horgan, Mr. B's personal assistant, as well as Eddie Bigelow and Lincoln Kirstein, went to Europe to persuade him to return to New York.[23] Mr. B then lavished his attention on Kay Mazzo, which made us all a little uncomfortable. It was a tension-filled time in the company.

I suppose people who are not familiar with Mr. B's relationships with the women in the company might easily look upon his behavior negatively. I saw his behavior as inherently human, as a man, and a way of connecting with the women who were part of his artistic vision for the company. His behavior made sense in a strange way. Mr. B loved women, and he surrounded himself with beautiful girls. He loved our talent and how our bodies could represent his choreography, and he was always there to help us. We were a family, with Mr. B as our leader.

He liked one-on-one conversations. He always called his dancers "dear," and he always had time to talk to us. He enjoyed having us come to him with our problems. He was very involved with pretty much all of us, even the dancers in the back line of the corps. He particularly enjoyed talking to the women in the company about their personal lives, like about boyfriends. "Have affairs, dear, but don't get married" was one of his standard pieces of advice. He liked to be consulted. He felt he could handle all our problems. He would say, "What do you need a psychiatrist for? You have me!" He just loved being around beautiful dancers.

It is a curious paradox to think that here was this man, this great genius. Why didn't he surround himself with scholars? Poets? Musicians? Why was he most comfortable surrounded by his young female dancers? But even with all of us around him, he seemed quite isolated, I guess because of his singularity as the company director. I often wondered what Mr. B did in his spare time, and throughout my time in the company, I was surprised to observe what a lonely man he seemed to be.

My relationship with Mr. B was always good. He often kidded with me, and since he was an extremely shy man, I felt flattered that he could talk to me. Although he was refined and cultured, he could be bawdy sometimes and would often tell little off-color jokes in company class. None of this shocked me because I never thought of him as evil or destructive. He had an elegance and a gentlemanly carriage at all times, although I was aware of the rumors of him having affairs with other company members.

Occasionally, Mr. B would invite me to dinner. I declined except when he invited another dancer to make a threesome. I just didn't want to be alone with him. I guess I was afraid we'd wind up staring at each other across the table, neither of us knowing what to say. Or perhaps I was afraid he would make a pass at me. I wanted to be rewarded for my talent and loyalty, but not because I had allowed him to touch me, which I thought might happen if I had dinner with him alone. I just didn't want to be in the position of accepting or rejecting his advances. However, I never did go to dinner with him alone, so I do not know what might have transpired.

Once, on tour in the States, we were staying at a motel. I had been to dinner after a performance with friends, and I walked up the stairs to my room. As I passed one of the other rooms, I saw the door was open, and I saw Mr. B lying on the bed in his underwear watching TV. It was a very hot night, and I think the hotel must not have had air-conditioning. When he saw me, he motioned for me to come in. I sensed he was probably lonely and wanted company, but I just couldn't do it, concerned again that I would find myself in a compromising position. What I wanted from Mr. B was just to have wonderful opportunities to dance. In this instance, he was not waiting for me to come by—it could have been any of the dancers in the company who walked by. And, who knows? Maybe he just wanted someone to talk to. I do want to emphasize here that it never even occurred to me that I *needed* to have an affair with him to get roles. I don't think that was a part of how he ran the company, and I certainly was given some wonderful roles without accepting any advances from him.

One of my more memorable experiences at NYCB was performing *Serenade*. I never did one of the three leads, but I was in the Russian dance for five women. If I ever felt spiritual, it was dancing this ballet. It is a joyous dance to perform. There is a tremendous amount of running, with the dancers just sweeping across the stage in various patterns. Mr. B created the first version of this dance in 1934 for some of his first students in the United States. It was performed on the Warburg estate

Serenade, 1963. *From left*: Lynda Yourth, me, Melissa Hayden, Rosemary Dunleavy, and Victoria Simon. Photo by Martha Swope ©Billy Rose Theatre Division, The New York Public Library for the Performing Arts.

in Westchester, on a platform erected on the lawn. Mr. B wasn't trying to create a masterpiece, just working to teach the students how to be on stage. The choreography seems to hint at a love triangle, but he meant it as pure movement. The story often told as to how the ballet was created is that there were often students absent from rehearsals, and he would just choreograph for whoever was there that day, so the numbers of dancers dancing are always changing. One dancer fell during a rehearsal, and he kept it in the dance. One dancer ran in late, and he used that in the dance. The Russian Dance has a gesture of the hand touching the forehead several times. We called it the Aspirin Dance. I loved per-

Serenade, circa 1966. I am on the far right; Delia Peters is in the foreground with Kay Mazzo behind her. Photo by Martha Swope ©Billy Rose Theatre Division, The New York Public Library for the Performing Arts.

forming *Serenade*, and I love watching it as an audience member. The final moment, when a lone woman is held aloft and carried offstage, always makes me tear up.

I also loved dancing *Concerto Barocco*. I was in the revival of it in the early 1960s. It is another of his dances that has a religious, spiritual feeling to me, dancing to that beautiful music, Bach's *Double Violin Con-*

certo. I'm not sure how to define it exactly, but that's how it felt. The magnificent choreography feeds your soul.

In addition to the ballets I have already mentioned, I was in the first movement of *Western Symphony* (in the corps when I first joined the company, and later I had the lead in the first movement). I was an understudy for both *Movements for Piano and Orchestra* (1963) and *Brahms-Schoenberg Quartet* (1966) as Mr. B was choreographing them. Although I did not dance in the premières, I eventually performed in them both.

I also performed *Episodes* (1959), *La Valse* (1951), and *Donizetti Varia-*

Brahms-Schoenberg Quartet, second movement, 1970. *From left to right*: Teena McConnell, me, and Sara Leland. Photo by Martha Swope ©Billy Rose Theatre Division, The New York Public Library for the Performing Arts.

Donizetti Variations, circa 1961. I am on far left, Edward Villella in center, and Suzanne Farrell on far right. Photo by Fred Fehl. Photo courtesy Gabriel Pinski.

tions (1960). I was in *Allegro Brillante* (1956), which I absolutely loved. In *The Four Temperaments* (1946), I performed as one of the two demi-soloists in "Melancholic" and one of four women in the "Phlegmatic" section. Although I was not in the premieres of these ballets, it was still often a creative experience to be cast in them and rehearse them. Mr. B attended rehearsals, and he would change choreography for various dancers. There is often not one "correct version" of a solo for instance, because he would alter choreography to fit each new performer of the role.

We used to joke about Melissa Hayden saying, "It was never like that!" about a particular sequence or step in one of the ballets. Not sure it was she who said it, but we would attribute that to her, and it was certainly something we all felt on occasion. Billy Weslow could really do Millie's voice and mannerisms perfectly. He was the great "imitator" of the com-

Donizetti Variations, circa 1966. *Back row from left to right:* Suzanne Farrell, Richard Rapp, Marnee Morris. *Front row from left to right:* Carol Sumner, Earle Sieveling, and me. Photo by Fred Fehl. Photo courtesy Gabriel Pinski.

pany, and he would say the most outrageous things and mimic people perfectly. He would do these imitations in class before Mr. B would come in, and I would laugh hysterically. Billy was truly one of a kind. I once had a purple coat, and with it I wore a black turban. Billy told me I looked like the actress Gene Tierney with my overbite and high cheekbones. I was flattered.

The Nutcracker season was a mainstay for the company. I danced so many roles in the annual run through the years. In the Party Scene, I performed the role of the mother. It required acting ability, which I had honed as a child actor but used less frequently in my ballet career. In Act II, I performed a range of roles: corps member or demi-soloist in

The Four Temperaments, circa 1969. Arthur Mitchell and me in foreground with Lynne Stetson to Mitchell's left. Photo by Martha Swope ©Billy Rose Theatre Division, The New York Public Library for the Performing Arts.

"Waltz of the Flowers" also called "Waltz of the Candy Flowers," the lead in "Marzipan," and the female lead in Spanish "Hot Chocolate." Anna Kisselgoff reviewed a *Nutcracker* performance on December 6, 1968, and wrote, "Gloria Govrin (Coffee), John Prinz (Candy Cane), Deni Lamont (Tea), Sara Leland (Marzipan), and Bettijane Sills and Earle Sieveling (Hot Chocolate) danced with style in the divertissements."[24] The Spanish costumes were beautiful, with so much detail. Barbara Karinska's dresses were partly velvet and had an underskirt, and the lead woman's costume even had a small cameo of Mr. B. But they weighed a ton, and it made turning almost impossible. You would go one way, and the skirt would go another! This was unusual for Karinska's costumes, as they were generally very easy to dance in. She put so much care into each one. She supervised all fittings. (Mr. B was often at them, too.) She was small and trim and usually wore a purple suit that matched her purple hair!

It was during *The Nutcracker* one Christmas season when I experi-

"Snow" from *The Nutcracker*, circa 1962. I am on the left in the front of the photo. Photo by Fred Fehl. Photo courtesy Gabriel Pinski.

enced my first real setback. I had learned the role of the lead Marzipan Shepherdess and was scheduled for six performances. I was having some trouble with the final pirouettes and, in my anxiety, had developed a "block" against them. Each performance became harder and harder, and after about the fourth performance, I decided to ask Mr. B if he would change the ending of the variation for me. I approached him and before I could ask him, he told me he was taking me out of the role. I was glad, in a way, because I had never felt right in the role when I rehearsed it, but I said to Mr. B: "Why did you cast me then, only to take me out?" I felt so ashamed. "Well, dear," he said, "I try different people—if they're not right, I take them out. I can be wrong. Besides, you're too heavy." Of

"Waltz of the Candy Flowers" from *The Nutcracker*, circa 1962. I am standing at the front on the left of the photo; Violette Verdy is in the middle as the Dewdrop Fairy. Photo by Fred Fehl. Photo courtesy Gabriel Pinski.

course, this was a blow. I was embarrassed to face the rest of the company. I felt they were all talking and whispering about me, and I knew the only way I could face coming to class every morning was to starve myself. So, for the umpteenth time, I vowed that *this* would be my thin season, and Mr. B would never have cause to take me out of a role again.

I was in the original cast of *Who Cares?*, which premiered in February of 1970 and was a highlight of that year for me in the company. Critic Marcia B. Siegel captured a key quality of the ballet: "With its Gershwin songs, cheerleader costumes, and jazzy-balletic movement it could so easily be pure kitsch. But it isn't because it's quite serious about the well-bred sweetness of the dancing that thousands of little girls in the thirties absorbed from Fred Astaire movies and mediocre dancing schools."[25]

The Nutcracker, Act II finale: Me dancing the lead in "Hot Chocolate" (Spanish Dance) with Robert Rodham (far-right front couple), beside the Sugar Plum Fairy (Patricia McBride) and her Cavalier (Edward Villella) (center front couple), and the lead in "Coffee" (Arabian Dance) (Francisco Moncion) partnering Dewdrop (Gloria Govrin), the lead in "The Waltz of the Candy Flowers" (far-left front couple), circa 1963. Photo by Fred Fehl. Photo courtesy Gabriel Pinski.

Ponytails with bows were the hairdo of choice once again, this time off to the side. Sometimes, when I had to perform a ballet before *Who Cares?* I was able to leave my hair in a bun so as not to take the time to fix my hair in a new style. I had a brief pas de deux, originally with Earle Sieveling, in the section "That Certain Feeling," but my larger role was the middle girl of the five in the "Somebody Loves Me" section. All of us danced much of the same choreography, but, since I was in the middle, I was featured. Originally the dance was very long, with double pirouettes and special steps that showed my strengths and personality. Once again, rehearsals were fun yet challenging in terms of stamina, but the steps came easily to me and suited my way of moving. Then Mr. B cut it down. I never knew for sure, and I never asked him, but I always suspected that it had to do with my weight again. We filmed *Who Cares?* in Canada, and when I watched it I saw the camera angles not focus on me as the middle girl but instead on the other four girls. I am sure that he was displeased with my weight at that time and purposely had the camera avoid lingering on me, despite my being the featured soloist in that section.

On December 3, 1970, I performed in the premiere of *Tschaikovsky Suite No. 3* in the "Elegie" section. The movement was lush and feminine with intricate, expressive arm gestures, and we wore no shoes. I never felt comfortable completely shoeless, so I asked if I could wear a little half sandal that gave my feet some support. Nobody minded and the sandal was barely noticeable. We also danced with our hair loose, so every dancer who performed one of the parts in the "Elegie" section had to have long hair. Mr. Balanchine loved to watch us dance with our hair unbound. Our costumes were on the order of *Serenade*, only in purple with jewels on the bodice. I was part of a corps of six women. I bought the recording and listened to it over and over, which I did a lot with many ballets. I loved dancing "Elegie" and have staged it a number of times for my students at Purchase College. While there is a sentimentality to this section of the ballet, I have always found it moving. There is a freedom and abandon, but while it may appear that there is no specific choreography, there are defined steps and patterns. A theme in this ballet, which is a recurrent theme in many Balanchine ballets, is loss—loss of the woman who, for the briefest of time, is his. He searches for her in the beginning and finds her, only to lose her in the end—the story of Mr. B's life, really. In Clive Barnes's review, he notes the originality of the first movement, "Elegie," describing its uniqueness for having the women in bare feet. He continues, "Six girls, led by Karin von Aroldingen and Anthony Blum, swirl around to the music, adopting attitudes but never taking sides. . . . Perhaps all of New York City Ballet should toss off their shoes. Those kids were beautiful."[26] This was not actually the first Balanchine ballet where there were dancers in bare feet; for instance, we also had bare feet in several sections of *Ivesiana*, but it was certainly not the norm for this company.

As I moved along in my career, new girls were always coming into the company, and it was interesting to observe them in action. They seemed to have very little respect for the older dancers of the company (of which

I was one by this time although only in my late 20s), and consequently were none too popular with us "old bags." It was strange to see the passage of time go so quickly. A ballet dancer's career is usually quite short, and Mr. B was particularly obsessed with youth.

Mr. B could take an interest in the weirdest types. Sometimes it seemed as if the stranger looking, the better. When we were in the company, there were many different body types, although he did want us all thin. But there were dancers in the company then who would never get in now. I don't think he was looking for cookie-cutter dancers. He wanted people he thought were interesting. He often told me I should develop a trick of some kind, turning, mannerisms, anything to make me different. "A dancer has to disturb me, make me itch," he said. It seemed to me sometimes that if you were just a plain, ordinary, good dancer you didn't stand a chance, but that is not really true. I had many wonderful roles. During my thinnest period, I was asked by the ballet mistress which ballets I wanted principal roles in. I thought about it and told her that the one role I would love to learn was the Coquette in *La Sonnambula*, but it never came to be. It would have been an opportunity to use my acting ability. I can't remember if I asked to learn anything else or not. I was just so thrilled and honored that Mr. B said I could have my choice. I knew I didn't need a trick to make me interesting. I would be rewarded directly as a result of my having lost weight, and because he liked my dancing. I want to stress that I did look gorgeous when I lost those extra pounds. I moved more easily and felt good about myself. I wasn't anorexic. I ate well. I just stayed away from sweets and carbs (except a baked potato now and then, no butter or sour cream), and I lost the weight slowly over time. But I gained most of it back on the layoff.

During the fall of 1970, the New York City Ballet Orchestra went on strike, which caused a cancelation of almost a month of our fall season. The dancers did not strike. The administration kept the dancers occupied by doing archival filming of various ballets in practice clothes. There is a film of me doing one of the variations from *Raymonda Variations*. We also filmed *Concerto Barocco* and the "Diamonds" section of *Jewels*.

In May of 1971, I met my first husband on a blind date arranged by fellow NYCB dancer Lynne Stetson and her husband, Dr. David Forrest.

At the time, Dr. Forrest was in training to become a psychiatrist, and he had a Jewish doctor friend, also a psychiatrist. Lynne and David knew I was Jewish, and they asked me if I wanted to meet someone. His name was William Rosenthal, and he was studying at Columbia University, as was David. We became serious quite quickly.

That fall of 1971, I went into Mr. B's office, and I told him I was getting married, and he said, "Dear, I hope you don't have a baby." I reassured him that I had no plans at that moment to have a baby, which, at that time, was true. I wanted to continue to dance. Mr. B used to say, "Don't get married, dear, have boyfriends. When you get married you lose your identity as a dancer and become Mrs. Doctor or Mrs. Lawyer." He seemed to approve somewhat of marriages between two dancers but felt that a nondancer husband could never really understand a dancer's life, and the marriage would fail. Better not to marry at all, and certainly not to have babies.

Dancers today are more independent. They get married and have children and keep dancing, but it was a bit like the 1948 movie *The Red Shoes* when we were there. (When the dancer in the movie gets married she becomes completely torn between her passions for her dance career and for her marriage.) Allegra Kent seems to have bypassed the negativity about marriage and kids, as she had both and kept dancing right through her life as a wife and mother. Mr. B adored Allegra, and he nurtured her through some difficult personal issues. Melissa (Millie) Hayden also married and had children, as did Patty McBride and Karin von Aroldingen. Just after her baby was born, Karin was at home while we were on tour in the United States. There had been a lot of dancers with injuries, and the company needed her. Mr. B called her and asked her to come join us on tour. She came and danced even though she had just had the baby. Mr. B greatly appreciated that sense of loyalty to him and the company.

All these dancers (Allegra, Millie, Patty, and Karin) were principal dancers, and that probably made a difference. Corps members and even soloists were somewhat expendable. Allegra, Millie, Patty, and Karin had really paid their dues and shown their devotion and loyalty. Mr. B cared about them deeply, and they were also the stars of his ballets. But generally, Mr.

B expected a total allegiance to him, which meant no marriage and no babies. He would lecture us about this sometimes. I defied this "rule."

In November of 1971, Bill and I were married by a rabbi at the Hampshire House on Central Park South, and I thought, "This is it!" I was marrying a Jewish doctor. That had been my plan in the far reaches of my mind. I invited Mr. B to my wedding when I married Bill. He said he couldn't come, but, as I mentioned in the introduction, sent a case of red wine, Nuits-Saint-Georges, with a note enclosed which said only "Remember me." I was still performing with City Ballet at the time of our wedding, so we postponed our honeymoon until the layoff and then went to Puerto Rico.

After getting married, I continued to perform for seven more months, during which it became apparent to me that it was time to leave the company. Rosemary Dunleavy, the ballet mistress, took me aside and told me that Mr. B no longer wished to encourage me, and I should find something else to do. I knew he had lost interest in me. The weight issue, of course, was major. I was not consistent in keeping my weight down. I would lose and he would reward, and then I would gain and he would take me out of roles. He liked my dancing, and I knew that. He was patient for many years, but he finally lost patience. I know I had disappointed him. He would have given me more roles to dance if I had kept my weight consistent. I am talking about a fluctuation of maybe five to ten pounds, but it made a difference. So I do have regrets. "You want to have a life outside of the company," Mr. B said to me, "and if your life makes you unhappy, you eat. Do you think anyone here is happy? You must learn to separate your life as a dancer from your outside life. Your responsibility is to yourself as part of the company, and while you are here, you must be thin. But I am patient—I can wait." I knew all this, and yet I couldn't seem to stop myself from binge eating. Although I had a wonderful career and danced many solo and principal roles and worked with the greatest choreographers of the twentieth century, I will always regret that I didn't stay thin for Mr. B and for myself.

In 1971, toward the end of my time at NYCB, and around when I got married, Mr. B came to a rehearsal of *Allegro Brillante*, and I was dancing my brains out. I knew he was watching me, and I knew what was going to happen. I was taken out of *Allegro Brillante* and *Concerto Barocco*. I was called to rehearsals to teach my parts to other dancers, like Debbie Flomine. It was awful. I was so self-conscious about how I looked that I asked to be taken out of *Movements for Piano and Orchestra* where the costume was white leotards. I was glad to be out of that, but Mr. B left me in *Agon*, which the women in the cast performed in black leotards and pink tights. I had gotten into *Agon* soon after I joined the company, and I danced it for eleven years as one of the four corps girls. I often wondered why he left me in it. He could be perverse. I was still able to dance confidently in the ballets in which I appeared in the longer tutu, like *La Valse*, where my thighs did not show so much, but less so in the leotard ballets. It was, however, extremely painful to be taken out of ballets that I loved to dance, and to be called to a rehearsal to teach my roles to some new, young thing.

I was originally cast in Mr. B's 1971 ballet about the airline company Pan Am—*PAMTGG*, standing for that company's marketing slogan at the time, "Pan Am Makes the Going Great." Merrill Ashley and I were clouds along with a group of dancers. There was one rehearsal where the clouds were not doing much, and Merrill and I went up to Mr. B, and she said, "Mr. B, can the clouds go?" We still laugh about it when we see each other. Anyway, as rehearsals progressed, my partner was having trouble lifting me, so Mr. B took me out. He thought I was too fat. But, in a way I am glad I was taken out, because it turned out to be one of his least successful ballets ever, and the dancers knew it was not going to be a masterpiece, even in rehearsals. Mr. B was choreographing a busy scene at an airport to a score by Roger Kellaway based on Pan Am's jingles. As Clive Barnes wrote, "This one hit rock bottom with the dull thud of ineffable triviality."[27] Marcia Siegel declared, "PAMTGG is not a ballet, it's a commercial."[28] It was not one of Mr. B's greatest moments. In the end, I considered myself lucky to be out of it, but not for the reason I was taken out. I was horribly embarrassed.

Having been told that Mr. B "wants you to think about finding something else to do," what was I going to do? I could have stayed, but I was taken out of my favorite ballets, and I knew he no longer intended to give me new things to dance. I remember my husband Bill and I invited Rosemary Dunleavy to dinner right before I left, at Bill's suggestion. He said to her, "Why did you fire my wife?" I don't remember how she answered. Of course, it wasn't really her decision, and I wasn't really fired. Bill was hurting because I was hurting. I remember asking Mr. B if I could have my old roles back if I lost the weight and kept it off, but he had moved on, and I needed to do the same. He was patient from 1961 to 1972. That is a long time. He was done, and so was I. I had a wonderful career, but I do have regrets that I was not able to make that total commitment.

In the last year, however, I did get one plum role from Jerome Robbins. Jerry returned to NYCB in 1969 as ballet master, and his involvement had a very positive effect on my later years with the company. His return may have been in part because of Mr. B's utter distress over Suzanne's marriage and departure from NYCB. Mr. B had an uncharacteristic "dry" period just after Suzanne Farrell left, and he didn't choreograph much, but the company needed choreography. Ballet was Jerry's first love, and he came back to it after working on Broadway. He had incredible sensitivity to the human condition and a wonderful comedic sense. Like Balanchine, music inspired him, but he also worked in silence. He was a master of the art of partnering; his ballets were filled with innovative pairings, lifts, and relationships. There was often a sense of genteel community among the dancers, perhaps after a moment of turmoil, as in *Dances at a Gathering*. Ballets such as *The Cage*, *Interplay*, *Fancy Free*, and *Fanfare* are timeless works.

I performed *Interplay* (1945), *The Cage* (1951), and *Fanfare* (1953), but I was not in the original casts. John Taras cast me and supervised the rehearsal period for these ballets. *Interplay* was one of the hardest ballets I have ever danced. We had to do a cartwheel, and I had to practice that on my own. Jerry came to watch rehearsal, and I feared that he would take me out of the ballet, but he didn't. Sometimes when I see photographs of me in that ballet I can't really believe that I danced such difficult choreography. In *Fanfare*, John cast me as a Horn, then a Violin, and finally I danced the Viola Pas de Deux with Roland Vazquez.

In preparation for his ballets for the next season, Jerry often asked us if we would be around during a layoff period. He wanted to work

Jerome Robbins's *The Cage*, circa 1962. *Back row from left to right:* Suzanne Farrell, me, Janet Greschler. Photo by Fred Fehl. Photo courtesy Gabriel Pinski.

with dancers and get a head start. I always was available and worked on *The Concert* and *The Goldberg Variations* during these times. Jerry began rehearsing *The Concert* in the summer of 1971. He originally choreographed it in 1956, but he was bringing it back into the repertory. Jerry liked me and appreciated my acting ability, for which I was extremely grateful. I had once told Mr. B that I had been a child actress and that, if

Jerome Robbins's *The Concert*, 1971. *From left to right*: me, Francisco Moncion, Sara Leland, and Steven Caras. Photo by Martha Swope ©Billy Rose Theatre Division, The New York Public Library for the Performing Arts.

he needed me for any roles that required acting ability, I was available. But Jerry's revival of *The Concert* really gave me the opportunity to show my sense of timing in a comedic role as "The Wife."

The role of "The Wife" was supposed to go to Violette Verdy. Jerry often would have one dancer learn a role and then teach it to another dancer who would ultimately perform that role. Violette was not around that summer as we began rehearsals, so I was to learn the part and then teach it to her. But when it came time to do that, Jerry seemed to prefer me, so I wound up with a principal role. I used to make him laugh in rehearsals, and that gave me great satisfaction. It was a role with a lot of comic possibilities. I felt appreciated for my acting ability, not only by Jerry but also by the various critics who reviewed the performances.

On December 4, 1971, Clive Barnes (the *New York Times*) called the ballet "a perfect gem," specifically stating: "The lovely cast was led by Sara Leland (an Isadora Duncan of a butterfly girl), Bettijane Sills, as a superbly pained House and Gardens, Book-of-the-Month Club wife, and Francisco Moncion as the malignant husband, hanging in there past his bedtime and still chewing his cigar."[29] Walter Terry, of the *Saturday Review*, wrote: "Bettijane Sills and Francisco Moncion were good as the battling married couple."[30] Joseph H. Mazo of *Women's Wear Daily* singled out Sara Leland, Francis Moncion, and me as being "very, very funny."[31] Jack Anderson wrote in *The Dancing Times* that "the cast was delightful," particularly calling attention to me as the "hatchet-faced wife."[32] Just a few months later Barnes wrote, "Bettijane Sills was still brilliantly unyielding as the stern and vinegary wife given over to good music and even better morality."[33]

Jerry also called me to the first *The Goldberg Variations* rehearsals earlier that same year. I was going to learn one of the leads, the same role as Gelsey Kirkland, and then my name disappeared from the rehearsal schedule. In the one rehearsal I had with Gelsey, Jerry spent most of his time watching her, and when the rehearsal was almost over, I sat down on the floor and took off my pointe shoes. He then asked me to show him the steps. I jumped up and danced without shoes. That was the end of it. I think Mr. B told him not to encourage me. I had a nice part in the ballet, but I did not dance a lead. *The Goldberg Variations* also premiered in 1971. Walter Terry praised Robbins and the dancers:

> I notice now that I have mentioned only two principal dancers, but this was done simply "for example"; all twelve featured dancers and the twenty-plus supporting artists are equally important in a superb ballet best described [by] an unidentified voice sitting somewhere near me on opening night: "It's perfectly simple to explain. Robbins is a genius, that's all."[34]

It was glorious movement to dance.

Rehearsals with Jerry were always a bit nerve-wracking as his own insecurities were palpable, and his anxieties affected his moods. He could be cutting and sarcastic at times, saying some mean things to his dancers. He was known for that, but I never felt that from him, which was very unusual. However, he did agonize over every step. We spent a lot of time on what could be termed minutiae and, unlike Mr. B who worked very quickly and allowed us a certain freedom with his choreography, Jerry reduced every movement to mind-numbing detail. His rehearsals could be tedious, and he often could not decide which version of his choreography he liked. He was constantly changing things: version one, version two, version three, and then he would go back to version one. Occasionally, there would even be a two-A and a two-B, and so on. You had to be on your game because sometimes we wouldn't know which version we were dancing until right before the curtain went up. There was a group of us informally known as Jerry's dancers, and we were all skilled at remembering the details of all the different variations. It could be confusing. But, to his credit, he knew exactly what he wanted—it was just a matter of getting there. His artistic sensibilities were impeccable; and yet, despite his many successful ballets, he seemed insecure and plagued by his many personal demons.

Jerry's pure-dance ballets, at least the ones I danced, did not necessarily produce that same feeling in me as dancing Mr. B's works, but I loved dancing his ballets, and I really enjoyed working with him. I remember once passing O'Neals' restaurant and seeing Jerry through the window sitting alone at a table. He motioned for me to come in, and I motioned back that I had somewhere to go. I regret very much not having gone in and sat with him. I do think he liked more about me than just my dancing.

The Stravinsky Festival ran from June 18 to 25, 1972, at the end of my time with the company. It was a spectacular event—the first of its kind for NYCB. Stravinsky had died just the year before, and 1972 was the ninetieth anniversary of his birth. For the festival, there were twenty-two new works to Stravinsky's music by Mr. B and other choreographers— Todd Bolender, John Clifford, Lorca Massine, Jerome Robbins, Richard Tanner, and John Taras.[35] Repertory works were also presented. In a way, it heralded that Mr. B was back as a major choreographic force after his short period of barely choreographing and the fiasco of *PAMTGG*.

In 1937, Balanchine had choreographed the full-length *Le Baiser de la Fée* to Stravinsky's score. For the festival, he reworked a part of it with the title *Divertimento from "Le Baiser de la Fée."* I was a soloist paired with Carol Sumner. The choreography was lovely and very inventive, but my head was in a very different place by that time, as I was already moving toward leaving the company, so I would say it was not my most enjoyable experience working with Mr. B. Arlene Croce wrote of the ballet in 1974: "The *Divertimento* is one of the most superbly crafted pieces to have come from Balanchine in recent years, and [Patricia] McBride, [Helgi] Tomasson, and the girls always perform it with exceptional polish, but it's basically footnote material, a collection of thoughts about a lost work of art."[36]

I also danced in the premiere of a ballet by Todd Bolender called *Serenade in A.* Todd had been assigned this music by Mr. B.[37] The ballet had some very difficult partnering, but it was not overly memorable.

I left the company right after the festival ended. They were getting ready for another tour to the Soviet Union. I had been there in 1962 and did not want to go again without my husband Bill, and he could not go. I was married, and my allegiance had changed. I danced my farewell performance, and my friends in the dressing room (Gloria Govrin, Carol Sumner, and Teena McConnell) bought me a lovely pair of earrings.

These days, Gloria Govrin teaches at a school in Connecticut. She has recently sent some of her dancers to audition at Purchase College, where I teach. She always sends me an email that says to look out for them. But we are not really in touch other than that. I was quite friendly with Carol Sumner and taught at her school, American Ballet Academy, in Stamford, Connecticut, from 1984 to 1987, but I have lost touch with her. I haven't kept in touch with Teena either, although I did see her at a NYCB reunion performance some years ago. When I left the company, I was given severance pay. I had to wait to get my retirement money because the union (AGMA) was at that time in the process of negotiating to change the mandatory retirement age, which was 65. Clearly, dancers retire well before 65 and should not have to wait until then to get their retirement checks. And that was it for me with NYCB.

I continued to take class for a while, often with Robert Denvers, who had a studio in the West 60s, but I did not perform again except for a very few brief appearances in the 1980s with the Purchase College dancers. I just stopped cold turkey. I never wanted to dance with another company. I had danced with the top company in the United States and perhaps the world. I was a Balanchine dancer. Also, I felt that it was time for me to have a "normal life," and I wanted very much to have a baby.

I continued and continue to see some of the dancers I danced with, some more frequently than others. Once, on the bus, shortly after I had left the company, I saw one of our seamstresses named Tusia. She was the one who sewed our last names in our costumes, but she had always misunderstood my name to be Siltz instead of Sills. When she saw me on the bus, she exclaimed in her Russian accent, "Oh Siltz! Vot, you still exist?" as if by leaving NYCB I might just have evaporated!

I do go back and watch NYCB perform, have done so ever since I left the company. When Mr. B was still alive, I would go backstage and talk to him after a performance. Some performances have bothered me and still do, particularly when I watch ballets that I danced, and particularly since Mr. B's death. The ballets have been changed, or maybe it is more accurate to say they have evolved. I remembered Mr. B rehearsing me, so it is distressing to see the ballets not looking like they did when I was performing. I do know each of us who performed the ballets have our own specific memories. Some are aligned and some conflict. Mr. B often changed bits here and there as he rehearsed them over time and with different dancers. However, there are stylistic details that I feel are sometimes missing and that were consistent when he was alive and overseeing every production.

I came to know Mr. B quite well over those years, and yet, as often as I thought I could predict his actions, more often I couldn't. He would see potential in someone that no one else saw, and after a while suddenly we would all say—"He was right!" And sometimes he would be disappointed in his choice of the moment. Perhaps he had an image of her that she could never attain. Perhaps she was lazy and never worked in class. Then he would admit jokingly: "Even I can make a mistake sometimes."

I often felt angry with him, too. A man with such an incredible ego and such dominance: What right did Mr. B have to so much power? What right to move his people like pawns on a chess board? As the sole leader, he could make top-down decisions. He largely did things as he saw fit. Lincoln Kirstein (with whom I sometimes saw Mr. B arguing) was the general director, and there was the board. But thanks to Kirstein and how he set up the company, NYCB was Mr. B's. He was in charge of casting, teaching, and creating new ballets. He was the genius and the brilliance behind it. But, really, he was a benevolent dictator. He was not a phony exerting power. One must remember what he created. People respected him, and most of his decisions made sense. It was a family feeling that we still have. Mr. B was a father figure and also the genius; it was his company and his alone.

The company was his life, and he was at the theater every day. I used to ask him why he didn't go home to rest once in a while, and he said that there would be plenty of time to rest when he was dead. Although he did not need to bother himself with administrative work, the pressures of directing the artistic aspects had to have been enormous. All the dancers relied on him; his board relied on him; and the public did, too. He had unusual and pervasive nervous tics, and I wonder if that pressure didn't contribute to them. The big one was a nose twitch. You did not see the twitch when he was teaching or choreographing. It was mostly when he was talking. Mr. B was soft-spoken. He did not yell and scream even when he raised his voice somewhat. And he did not like confrontations. I think he largely left the difficult conversations (like Rosemary Dunleavy telling me that it was time for me to leave the company) to other people.

In some ways, I think that we sort of took Mr. B for granted. We knew we were in the presence of genius. We knew that what he did was special. There were some ballets that were not successful; you know everybody has a clunker now and then. But, for the most part, he was turning out masterworks every season and, of course, overseeing *The Nutcracker*, which had seemingly endless performances. I think it took his death to make me realize that I experienced what people are now calling "The Golden Years" (the 1960s) of NYCB. That was my time there. Looking back on it with the perspective I have now, I do realize that it was a very special time. We thought Mr. B was going to live forever and continue to create beautiful ballets. Perhaps that's why we didn't think that much about how extraordinary the time was; we thought it was just going to keep going. Then when he became ill and couldn't work anymore and just deteriorated, it was such a terrible shock for everybody—that world was coming to an end. Even to this day, when I walk by Lincoln Center, I expect to see him coming toward me in his raincoat. It is still hard, and he died in 1983.

I attended his funeral at a Russian Orthodox Church on the Upper East Side of Manhattan, the Cathedral of Our Lady of the Sign. It was so crowded that you couldn't move inside the church, and outside there was a huge crowd, too. There were so many familiar faces—teachers from the school and company members with whom I had danced.

Mr. B basically gave the company to Peter Martins at his death. Martins had been named ballet master in 1981, along with Mr. B, Jerry Robbins, and John Taras. When Mr. B died, Peter and Jerry became co-ballet masters in chief, but Peter was really in charge of day-to-day activities. It all came as a surprise to some people because there were other dancers Mr. B had groomed through the years with the possible idea of their taking over for him after he died. Mr. B was somewhat of a realist. He knew he was a kind of linchpin that could not just be replaced. He used to say, "Après moi, the board." I am sure he was looking in part for someone he thought could deal with the complicated structure of the company— more than just working with the dancers. In 1990, Peter assumed full directorship of NYCB.

Chapter 5

Teacher, Répétiteur, and Choreographer

After I left NYCB, in 1972, I went to Mr. B and told him of my interest in teaching at the School of American Ballet. I always thought that I would wind up working there, just as Suki Schorer, Kay Mazzo, and Susan Pilarre did. I thought surely he knew that I understood his style and technique and that he would welcome me to the faculty. He took me to see Mme. Ouroussoff, who was the executive director of the school, and said, "Bettijane wants to teach." Mme. Ouroussoff said very sweetly that there were no openings at that point. I think he just made a show of trying to accommodate me. I know if he had wanted me to teach there, he would have made it possible. To this day, I feel misunderstood by him in this regard. I feel I would have been an asset to the faculty at SAB. I think I understood what he wanted from the teachers at the school, but I don't think he saw that in me. I don't think he realized that I would have had something valuable and positive to offer the students. Perhaps his opinion of me was colored by the fact that I never fulfilled my potential in his eyes. After a while, I don't think he could get beyond that and see that I had something more to offer. On the other hand, his allowing me to teach at the school would have been a reward, and since he had run out of patience and moved on, I can understand his thinking, but I felt very disappointed at the time. As I look back now, I realize that my position at Purchase College has been very rewarding on many levels. I am a tenured professor with retirement and health benefits, and I work with incredibly talented students and faculty.

In terms of teaching at that time, however, I had other plans. I was already thirty, and I knew I wanted to have a baby. I'd been hearing stories about dancers having trouble getting pregnant, and I did not want to wait too long and increase the risk of having a baby with birth defects related to advanced maternal age, or just not be able to get pregnant. But I got pregnant pretty much right away after I left the company. People would ask me if being pregnant was hard because it changed the shape of my body, but I don't remember that as having been difficult, or that I had strong feelings about "body image." I was happy to be pregnant.

Former NYCB dancers Diana Adams and Patricia Wilde were teaching at Purchase College, State University of New York, around this time, about an hour's drive north of New York City. They were two of the first faculty members in the dance program. Sometime in the spring of 1973, while I was pregnant, I got a call from Diana, and she said to me, "I have an asthmatic daughter, and I might need to take her to the emergency room occasionally. Would you be available to teach at Purchase College, to 'sub' for me?" I said, "Yes!" I was very flattered. It would be the first time I would really be teaching. (Now that I think back, Mr. B may have told Diana I was looking for teaching work. They were always close.) I was still living in Manhattan, and although I was learning to drive, I did not yet have my license. The first time Diana needed a "sub," Kazuko Hirabayashi (another dance faculty member) picked me up in the city (we had not yet moved to Westchester) and drove me up to the college. Here was this tiny lady behind the wheel of this huge station wagon! Purchase College was still a construction site at that point. The dance building had not even been built, so the class was held in the gym. I had written down my combinations because I had never taught before, and I didn't want to forget anything. After that, I was called a couple of times to teach.

Bill and I had been living on East 78th Street and Third Avenue in a lovely one-bedroom apartment, but Bill wanted to leave the city, so we started looking in Westchester. We bought a house in Armonk, also about an hour's drive north of New York City and close to Purchase College, in a beautiful area called Windmill Farm. We paid $99,000 for that house, which is now probably worth three million. Every house in the area is on at least two-and-a-quarter acres. We moved to Armonk while I was still pregnant, and my son was born on Columbus Day, October 12, 1973. We named him Ben David Rosenthal. It had been a tremendous adjustment to leave the ballet company because it was my family, and having the baby was a huge adjustment, too, as was leaving the city. In

My son, Ben David Rosenthal, age 2, and me, 1975. Photo by Bill Rosenthal.

fact, I always considered myself a city girl and never thought I would ever wind up in the "burbs."

When my son was born, I stayed home and took care of him. Bill sometimes would say that he wished I would contribute financially to the marriage, so, around 1976, I organized a bit of teaching for myself in Armonk. I rented a large room in a nearby church and gave adult and children's ballet classes. I called the school the Bettijane Sills School of Ballet, but it was short-lived.

In 1977, I was invited by Allegra Kent, former NYCB principal dancer, to buy into her school, the Allegra Kent School of Ballet, which she had started in 1975.[1] It was in Scarsdale, which was conveniently close to where I was living. I thought this was a good situation but soon began to think otherwise.

I was teaching eleven classes a week, and I had never taught that much in my life. Most of these were children's classes, and I was not great at teaching little kids. Plus, I was doing payroll and bookkeeping, none of which I had done before. I did learn a lot, but the problem was that I was trying to do this without full-time child care and hiring baby-sitters piecemeal. My son was around four, very young. It was too much to juggle. So, when Allegra announced that she was selling her half of the school, I was faced with a decision. I could buy her out and be sole owner of the school, or I could sell my share as well. I had been in the business less than a year, but I decided to sell, and the school went on the market. William (Billy) Glassman, who was a dancer with American Ballet Theatre and with whom I had trained at SAB when we were children, ended up buying it. I was relieved to be out of that situation. I decided that I was not going to teach anymore, that I would devote myself to my marriage and my son.

Another enormous event in my life in 1977 was that my father passed away. He had had a stroke thirteen years earlier, but his heart finally gave out and he died of pulmonary edema. He was the first person I was close to who died. I had so many mixed feelings. My parents' unhappy marriage had been very hard on me, and my father's being away on tour so much left our relationship a bit more distant than my relationship with my mother. I finally realized I loved him very much, but I had feelings of anger toward him because he had been so nasty to my mother. He had his own personal demons, yet because of him there was always music in my house, and I particularly learned to appreciate classical music. I am so glad he got to meet his grandson.

As Ben got older we put him into soccer, the typical suburban sports thing, but he didn't seem particularly interested in sports. He also played the trumpet beautifully. Perhaps dancing lessons might have been good for him, but I didn't want to be like my mother, so I did not push him in any direction, something I find myself regretting at times. He was enrolled in the Coman Hill Elementary School, in Armonk, which turned out not to be the best environment for him. We then put him in private school, the Home School in White Plains. He did well there. There was a lot of one-on-one work with the teacher, and there were just seven or

My mother and me, swimming with my son, Ben, 1977. Photo by Bill Rosenthal.

eight kids in his class. He loved his teachers, and they loved him. He made friends. It was so much better, he seemed much happier, and it allowed me to begin to think about teaching again.

In 1979, I learned that Jacques d'Amboise had become dean of dance at Purchase College. We were still living in Armonk at that point. My mother said, "Why don't you call Jacques and tell him you're five minutes away, if he needs a 'sub.'" My mother was always thinking about my career. Some people might think she was interfering, but I am grateful for her never-ending ideas, which could further my career, this time my teaching career. So, I called Jacques. He said, "I am doing a summer program. I am hiring Carol Sumner, but I need another teacher, too. Can you come in to teach for three weeks?" I said, "Sure." After the summer program, he proceeded to offer me a full-time job as an assistant professor to replace Ann Parsons, who was leaving. He said, "We have to give a show of having a formal search, but I am going to offer you the position. It is yours if you want it." Wow! How could I turn that down? I started teaching at the college, and I have been there ever since. And I have Jacques to thank for that. And my mother.

Purchase College was founded in 1967, with the first full freshman class entering in 1972. It was designed to offer conservatory training in the visual and performing arts, as well as to offer liberal arts and sciences programs.[2] The School of the Arts comprises three conservatories: dance, music and theater arts, and a school of art and design. The arts students take ninety credits in their discipline and thirty liberal arts credits to graduate with a Bachelor of Fine Arts (BFA). For the students in the conservatory of dance, the goal is to become a professional ballet dancer, a modern dancer, or a choreographer. The students enrolled in the dance conservatory take ballet and modern dance all four years. They learn improvisation in their freshman year and take composition (choreography) for the subsequent three years, culminating in their senior project. Purchase College is one of the most successful public universities in the United States in terms of producing working artists in dance, theater, music, visual arts, and film. Graduates from the conservatory of dance perform with major companies in the United States and abroad, direct their own companies, and teach in various locations from studios to conservatories.

When Jacques came in as dean of dance at Purchase, in 1978, he was still busy with many projects in the city. He was continuing to perform, and he had his National Dance Institute. Because of his commitments, he was not at Purchase every day. He did choreograph a lot for the student concerts. He made dances for large casts and liked to get all the dancers on stage at once. Jacques was only at Purchase as dean of dance for two years. He left very soon after getting me appointed.

I came into an atmosphere in which there was some student resistance to ballet in general, and specifically Balanchine, and this affected the students' reaction to me. Rightly or wrongly, I think some of the resentment toward Balanchine stemmed from disapproval about the Balanchine "look" (long neck, long limbs, and very thin), which was adopted by large swaths of the dance community. So I was trying to teach classical dancing to a group of kids who harbored adverse feelings about New York City Ballet and, therefore, me. They were very disrespectful. There were boycotts of some of the performances we put on in my first year. They wrote articles in the student newspaper, telling other students not to go to the concerts. This negativity coincided with my efforts and my need to grow and develop as a teacher.

I did have some intellectual satisfaction in my early period of teaching, though. At my mother's suggestion, I had taken courses at Hunter College just after high school. In my first years at Purchase, I completed my undergraduate degree through Empire State College, again at my mother's suggestion. I have a BPS, a Bachelor of Professional Studies. I took terrific courses through Empire State, such as literature and film. They fed a different part of me from dance.

I had not been at Purchase for very long when my marriage began to fall apart, around 1982, when my son Ben was nine. When my marriage was good, I loved being married, but there were underlying problems from the start. One big issue was that my husband and I did not agree on methods of child-rearing. There were times when my husband would be ready to scold Ben, and I was ready to comfort him. It was not a healthy situation. As I look back on those years, I don't think I was mature enough or emotionally prepared to be married to a man like Bill. Bill was brilliant and funny, and I fell for his sense of humor. Yet I had not learned to stand up for myself and be my own person.

As Mr. B had warned, I lost my identity somewhat in this first marriage. I went back to see him later, after I had left the company, and told him that he was right, and he said, "See dear, you should have listened to me."

Ultimately, my marriage to Bill and subsequent divorce left me feeling demoralized. By the end, I had little sense of self-worth. The struggle to overcome this loss of self-confidence was slow, but bit by bit, I began to take control of my life. The chance to teach steadily, to bright and demanding students, was a major help. My career at Purchase College constantly challenged me to take on more and more in dance education, and as I confronted new challenges, I realized that I was becoming a very different person, a person who trusted her instincts and intelligence. I learned that my success, professionally and personally, depended on me. As long as I was willing to take risks, I could be successful in whatever I endeavored. This was a long learning process, though. And my son also suffered because of the divorce. He lived with me for a while and then with his father. Ben, a writer now, is married to my lovely daughter-in-law, Karen, and they have two sons, Henry and Quentin. I am very proud of him.

As I was going through the divorce and recovering from it, I was also working hard on developing my teaching. When I first came to Purchase, I was giving a Balanchine class, and the modern dancers didn't understand it. They didn't feel that this way of studying dance in the studio was something they wanted to do, and so there was a lot of negativity about the way I taught. I was a brand-new teacher, and my approach was not working well. I had to learn how to communicate better with the modern dancers, who tend to be more analytical and intellectual about things. When Jacques first hired me, he said that the Purchase students want to think about what they are doing, to analyze and talk about it. They want to approach ballet in an intellectual way. Now, if you do the leg movement of tendu with the requisite energy from in to out, you don't need to know the exact muscle you are using, but they want to know. They take anatomy and want to connect the two courses. I had to learn how to address that need when I first started teaching there. This was not the way I was trained—I was told, "Just do it!" If you were lucky and talented, you could learn to dance, but you didn't necessarily know which muscle you were moving or where the muscles were connected. A lot of the students also come from schools where they are encouraged to ask a lot of questions. Sometimes, having to stop the process of doing a movement to satisfy intellectual curiosity in the moment is too much. It is not good to ask a question after each combination, for instance; one loses momentum and energy. Students need to trust themselves in a ballet class, to understand that mistakes are okay, that mistakes are part of the learning process.

To begin to make changes, I worked very hard on watching my Purchase colleagues—like Rosanna Seravalli and Richard Cook, people whom I respected. I also learned to use humor in teaching because it helps the students and me. I realized what I needed to do, but at the same time I felt strongly that ballet should be taught as ballet, and I still feel that way. I am not an advocate of teaching ballet for modern dancers in a way that is watered down or diluted. Ballet should be taught as it is, maintaining high standards and the specific style. Often, I find my students approaching their ballet classes as a form of aerobics, just exercise to get warmed-up. Those students who are mostly modern-focused and have not had the best prior ballet training seem to have difficulty experiencing the beauty and freedom of moving through space in a ballet class. They are hampered by their lack of foundational technique. I look back on my strong training at the School of American Ballet and at the High School of Performing Arts as I teach my students. What I teach is really a compilation of all the training I have had from various teachers, who all contributed to make me the dancer I ultimately became. I like to tell stories from my training and performing days to my students, like the stories I have told in earlier chapters of this book. I even give combinations I remember from Pierre Vladimiroff's and Stanley Williams's classes.

Vladimiroff gave lovely combinations but rarely varied them. However, because we repeated them so often, I remember them exactly. They were difficult combinations and are quite challenging for my students.

Williams was a technique guru for many of the NYCB dancers (and even dancers from other companies). Stanley worked a lot on speed, as for very fast petite allégro combinations. He also contrasted fast and slow. As much of ballet classwork is focused on moving toward or away from your center, one of his favorite expressions was: "You're going out, now you have to go in." He was not teaching at SAB when I was there, but I did take his classes when I could after joining the company.

I would say that Balanchine shaped my aesthetic sensibility most profoundly, and I work to incorporate his theories into my classes. Teaching in a college dance program such as Purchase's conservatory of dance is very different from teaching in a conservatory such as SAB. And although modern dance has crept into the training of ballet dancers in some conservatories, Purchase offers a modern-focused program with a strong ballet component. Given the large number of modern dancers I teach at Purchase, it would not be prudent or productive to teach a purely Balanchine class. I'm not trying to create Balanchine dancers, but I do feel it is very important to stress elements of the technique that all my students can benefit from and that will strengthen their bodies and their understanding of Balanchine's aesthetic.

Mr. B expected and demanded that his dancers move bigger and faster with higher leg extensions (especially to the side) and to execute steps with ease and full range of motion. All these things could only be achieved by having a strong ability to rotate the legs outward, away from the body (turn-out) and by the understanding that 5th position is the beginning and ending of basic and advanced steps and choreography in classical ballet. The use of the "perfect" 180-degree outward rotation of the legs in 5th position serves to emphasize the inventive and often surprising images in Balanchine's neoclassical choreography during which the legs and feet might turn inward in opposition to the traditional turned out position.

Mr. B had specific demands for tendu (extending the working leg to the front, side, and back, touching the floor)—he wanted the leg in tendu front to be in line with the center of the body and not crossing over. Mr. B also wanted the weight slightly forward, so that dancers would be able to move quickly.

As well, his port de bras (movement of the arms) was very specific: The arms always rose up the center of the body; the hand was to end up over the center of the head wherever the head was inclined; and the arms had to have energy and purpose. Mr. B's favorite movie was the 1956 version of *Invasion of the Body Snatchers*. The movie tells the story of aliens who come from outer space and colonize the homes of the victims. They grow in the basements in large pods and eventually the pods hatch and the creatures inside are exact replicas of the people living in the homes. In other words, the real people now disappear only to be replaced by the pod people. Mr. B used to tell us that if we did our arm movements, our port de bras, in a disconnected way, then we looked as if we had become the pod people.

Teaching at Purchase College, 2017. Photo by Paige DeMaio.

One aspect of ballet training, which was stressed by all my teachers, including Mr. B, is the use of épaulement, the positioning of the shoulders, neck, and head. It becomes a real challenge as a teacher to try to get my students to understand that the inclination of the head is not merely a position but can be used to enhance the beauty of the art form while the body changes position as it moves through space. Some students enter Purchase without having been properly taught épaulement.

Mr. B also always wanted more energy, but clearly directed energy. He would say, "What are you saving yourself for? Do it now. Now is all there is." And he was right. I continually stress this with my students, and they begin to understand the use of energy while taking class. If they are using their energy correctly, it will automatically develop the muscles the way they need to be developed. They sometimes think they are working hard but are often not working how they need to work. In fact, I respond more to a student who may not have the best technique if he or she works with physical energy. Happily, stronger and better trained ballet dancers are entering our program lately, dancers who have the technique and strength to master the Balanchine choreography, despite not having been trained previously in the Balanchine style or technique.

But I do find today that there can often be misunderstandings of what Mr. B desired. An idea such as what he wanted with hands—strong, but natural and with five fingers showing—can start to look like a claw if his style is not fully understood. Or his idea of not putting the heels on the ground always or immediately when landing from jumps. This can be overdone with detrimental effects on student dancers.

I feel a great responsibility to impart his style and aesthetic in the way he intended. So, while I am not trying to turn my Purchase students into Balanchine dancers, I think it is important that they have the understanding and the ability to see that, according to what style of ballet one is learning, there are different ways of carrying your arms and different ways of executing a tendu: Balanchine's is one among a group of approaches—but it is the one I most value. Because of my experience working directly with Mr. B, I have an understanding of his way of working and teaching that I feel is important to give to the students. I just had to figure out how best to deliver that information because the Purchase dancers need a different delivery method from how I was taught. They particularly want more verbal information, so, in addition to detailed verbal descriptions of what I want them to do, I also like to tell my students little anecdotes from Mr. B's class. For instance, although we were already in the company and dancing technically well, there was always something more we needed to do to show Mr. B that we understood what he wanted. Often, with the utmost patience, he would correct a dancer over and over on the same step or port de bras until finally she "got it." When that happened he would say, "You see, I should have been a dentist!" "Why?" we would ask. "Because it's like pulling teeth!" This story always gets some chuckles. I love it because it illustrates Mr. B's passion, persistence, and patience.

Over time, I have become increasingly successful in developing my teaching methods for my college students. I have been told that, at big studios like Steps in Manhattan, my students are recognizable when they take open classes with other NYCB alums-turned-teachers because they have the Balanchine style. Francis Mason, noted dance historian and critic, once referred to me as the keeper of the Balanchine flame. I am very proud that he thought of me that way.

Through the years, I have worked with a number of deans of dance at Purchase. After Jacques, there were several people, Carolyn Brown being one, who stayed just a short while. Kazuko Hirabayashi was interim dean in the early 1980s. Kaz promoted ballet at the college even though she was a "modern" person. She encouraged me to stage *Serenade* for the first time, in 1983. The same year, I also came out of dance retirement and performed the role of the "doll" in our fund-raising production of Michel Fokine's *Petrouchka*. It was an incredible feeling to be dancing once more. I even lost the weight (finally) and dropped down to 111 pounds, thinner than I had ever been. I performed again, in 1984, in *Les Noces* (Bronislava Nijinska) with Purchase dancers, and in *S'Wonderful*, by Michael Vernon, at the Northern Westchester Center for the Arts Gala Benefit.

Carol Walker became dean of dance in 1984 and continued until 2007. Carol and I worked many years together and always got along well. She threw herself into this job, working unbelievable numbers of hours with so much care and concern for the students. We are still friends and see each other socially. I was tenured in 1996 and promoted to full professor in 2006 under Carol. She was followed by Carol Shiffman, and then Wallie Wolfgruber for short periods of time. I was interim co-director for a year in the transitional period after Wallie.

In the summers, I have taught students of different ages at many

Me as the doll in *Petrouchka* with Kevin Wynn at Purchase College, 1983. Photo by Scott E. Powell.

different schools: American Academy of Ballet, Ballet Academy East, Allegheny Ballet Summer Intensive, Central Pennsylvania Youth Ballet, Northern Westchester Center for the Arts, Scarsdale YMCA, the SUNY Youth Program, Lehman College Summer Arts Festival, Summer Ballet Intensive at Purchase, and North Carolina School of the Arts.

While developing my teaching skills, I also developed my skills as a choreographer. I choreographed a nice little ballet for the students the first year I was working at Purchase, and I found that I enjoyed it. I had received some criticism that I was not doing any work outside the university, so I got involved with the Carlisle Project, directed by Barbara Weisberger. The Carlisle Project ran from 1984 to 1996 and was dedicated to nurturing choreographic talent in ballet.[3] *New York Times* dance critic Gia Kourlas quoted Barbara: "'Why are we the only art form that says there's no craft?' she asked wearily. 'Of course there's a craft. It isn't stymieing anybody's gift. It's about nurturing.'"[4] And Barbara certainly nurtured me. I would go to Carlisle, Pennsylvania, for a week and would be provided with professional dancers, space, and time to choreograph, plus workshops on choreography. And they paid a stipend.

Through the years, I have choreographed various other ballets for the Purchase students and stayed involved with the Carlisle Project. In 1982, I choreographed *Slavonic Dances* for the Purchase students, and, in 1993, my ballet *Simple Symphony* had a very nice write-up by Jennifer Dunning in the *New York Times*. Dunning described *Simple Symphony* as having "all the enjoyable good-spiritedness" of my own dancing when I was a member of NYCB. In addition, she said that "Miss Sills has a sense of craft and has tailored the dancing to her dancers, giving them, it seems, what they do best without at all choreographing down to them."[5]

I choreographed a ballet called *Masquerade*, with music by Aram Khachaturian, for the Central Pennsylvania Youth Ballet in 2008. New Jersey Ballet then asked me to set it for their company, which was very exciting. The artistic director had seen it performed in Harrisburg, Pennsylvania. I had originally choreographed three movements, but they only amounted to about fifteen minutes, so the company asked me to choreograph two more movements for more money. A performance of *Masquerade* by New Jersey Ballet was reviewed by Robert Johnson in the *New Jersey Star Ledger*: "This tongue-in-cheek program reprised the troupe's Halloween season opener, with the addition of 'Masquerade'—a stylish company premiere choreographed by Bettijane Sills."[6] He continued:

> In "Masquerade," we seem to hear the rustle of silk and feel a
> cool breeze as two couples, a female soloist and a corps of eight

women in ball gowns waltz to a score by Aram Khachaturian. Like a dream, this ballet comes outfitted in elegant yet dusty trappings. Ambiguity creates an air of menace. In a central episode, two women—talented new company members Yuki Omori and Elisa Toro Franky—wear masks and switch partners. The soloist, striking Ekaterina Smurova, might seduce one or both of the men—or she might finish the evening plaintively alone. "Masquerade" isn't a ghost ballet, but it may make you shiver. Even the corps women have a terrific attack, seeming eager to throw themselves into the circling figures of the waltz.[7]

The ballet was performed at the New Jersey Performing Arts Center for a fundraising gala in 2010. There was a dinner after the performance, and a New Jersey Ballet board member made a speech thanking me for staging such a lovely Balanchine ballet. I admit to being very flattered that he thought *Masquerade* was a Balanchine ballet, and I figured I was in good company. I then set the ballet at Purchase.

I choreographed a senior project in the fall of 2014, a challenging tango ballet for a beautiful, statuesque young woman who graduated that December. I was given a "50 for 50, Arts Westchester" award in 2015 in recognition of my choreography. I plan to continue to choreograph. As a NYCB dancer, I was exposed daily to the genius of Mr. B's creativity. His impetus was always the music, and that is my impetus as well. A first step is usually finding a piece of music that inspires me. I saw Mr. B "visualize" the music through dance, and I try to do that, too, using the classical vocabulary to convey what I hear in the music. I have my own creative voice that I work to project in my choreography, but I also use the tools I learned through watching Mr. B. I don't choreograph "down" to dancers. I attempt to challenge them. I give them not only what they do best already but also what I know they *can* do, even if they do not know it yet, just as Mr. B did with me and my fellow dancers.

I have also been a répétiteur, staging quite a few Balanchine works at Purchase and elsewhere in cooperation at first with New York City Ballet and later with The George Balanchine Trust, which licenses Balanchine's ballets for performance. In 1983, I staged my first Balanchine choreography: the first three themes from *The Four Temperaments*, for the Purchase students. At that time, it was unheard of for NYCB to allow college students to perform Mr. B's work, and Purchase was the first college program to do so. Mr. B had never been a big fan of college dance programs. I know the permission to stage this meant the company, by way of Barbara Horgan (of George Balanchine's office), trusted me. In 1983, I also staged *Serenade.* It has a fairly large cast and complicated stage patterns. I wasn't sure how the Purchase students would handle it, but they were fantastic. They learned the patterns from the video, and then I worked extensively with them on style like the crossed fifth position, the bending body and head, and Mr. B's very fast footwork.

In 1984, I staged Balanchine's second (1967) *Valse Fantaisie,* to music by Mikhail Glinka. Purchase graduate Nancy Turano remembers that we toured it around to eight of the State University of New York (SUNY) schools and that it was a formative and important first experience of

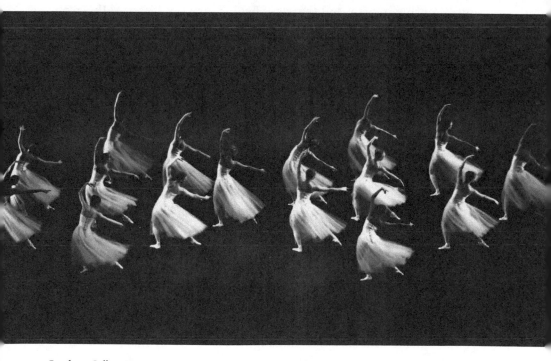

Purchase College Dancers in *Serenade,* 2004. Photo by Ted Kivitt.

touring.[8] It also gave students at other SUNY schools the opportunity to see Balanchine's work. The choreography is complex and takes great technical skills. It was an honor for the Balanchine Trust to allow us to perform the work. In 1987, I staged it again for the Purchase students, and we traveled to Hong Kong and Macau to perform it.

My staging of the "Elegy" section of *Tschaikovsky Suite No. 3* for Purchase students, in 1991, was reviewed by Jennifer Dunning in the *New York Times*: "Staged by Bettijane Sills, the ballet was danced with attention to detail and an underlying innocence that is embedded in the work but seldom revealed so clearly."[9] I am exceptionally proud of this review because Dunning emphasized key aspects of the dance that were a major focus in our rehearsal process.

Another particularly memorable event was staging *Serenade* for my Purchase students in 2004. We performed the dance at the high school that was built on the grounds of the former Warburg estate, in the hamlet of Greenburgh, New York, where *Serenade* was first performed. Our performance was part of the celebration of the hundredth anniversary of Balanchine's birth, and therefore held special significance. This wonderful ballet, commissioned as a birthday present for Lincoln Kirstein's friend Edward Warburg by his parents, was physically brought back to the location of its world première. Anna Kisselgoff wrote of the performance, "Bettijane Sills, a former dancer in City Ballet, instilled her staging with the impetus of youth and freshness."[10]

A critic from the online magazine the *DanceView Times* also attended the performance and captured the poignancy of the event. The ballet was choreographed for a cast partially made up of students, who have a different look from professionals, and here it was being performed by students on a stage about the size of the original, located just about on the spot of that first outdoor stage. She wrote:

> The platform would not have been very large, and it was instructive to watch a performance of *Serenade*—staged with sharp attention to detail by NYCB alumna Bettijane Sills for student dancers of the SUNY/Purchase conservatory program—in the similarly constrained auditorium of the high school's nearby main building. Compressed in space, the ballet's energy intensified; and seeing it at

such close range, one was reminded of how thoroughly the theme of being a student permeates the choreography. Professional dancers in *Serenade* are thinner, stronger, perhaps more virtuosic, but they don't have the look of complete commitment to a mortal challenge and mysterious process that dedicated students do. To truly see *Serenade* in its letter and its spirit, I think, one must see youngsters, with their entire lives and hopes before them, perform it. Only then do its most melancholy ironies, the retrospective elements that the choreographer built into the work, surge forth with stinging clarity.[11]

Other Balanchine ballets I have staged at Purchase are *Concerto Barocco, Tarantella, The Steadfast Tin Soldier,* excerpts from *Stars and Stripes, Scotch Symphony*, and excerpts from *Who Cares?* In the spring of 2016, I staged the full version of *The Four Temperaments*. Some of my stagings have been for main concert productions and others for senior projects. The senior project for Dance at Purchase is a combination of the student's performance of a piece by an established choreographer in the field and the student's own work for five or more dancers. For the "established choreographer" part, the students ask a choreographer to choreograph a work on them, or they get permission to perform a dance that has already been made. They perform these works (about five students on each program) in their own concerts, which they organize themselves and for which they get the necessary permissions. The Balanchine Trust is wonderful in not charging royalties for senior projects, since they are not public performances.

Outside of Purchase, I have staged Balanchine ballets widely: *Serenade* for the Philadelphia School of the Arts, the Taipei National University of the Arts, and the Hong Kong Academy for the Performing Arts; *Valse Fantaisie* for the Allegheny Ballet Company and the New England Dance Theatre; *Allegro Brillante* for the Orlando Ballet in Florida; the "Elegy" from *Tschaikovsky Suite No. 3* for the Columbus Youth Ballet and Martha Graham II; the concert version of *Who Cares?* for the Allegheny Ballet Company; excerpts from *Stars and Stripes* for Repertory Dance Theatre (Allentown, Pennsylvania); and excerpts from *The Nutcracker* for Stamford City Ballet. In staging Mr. B's dances, I work from video and from memory if it is a work I performed. The Balanchine

Trust doesn't send hard-copy videos anymore. They send a link to a digital video and give a password.

As a stager (or répétiteur) of his work, I am passing on Mr. B's legacy. I love being able to share what I remember from rehearsals with Mr. B—what he told us and how he wanted us to dance. I think that information is so important from a pedagogical point of view. His legacy is more than the steps that form a ballet. A choreographer's style is in the details and the specific way and approach to doing steps. I don't think Mr. B ever envisioned his ballets to be used in the pedagogical sense, but they are wonderful educational tools. The dancers improve when they dance his work: They begin to understand the technique and stylistic details from inside the choreography, rather than just following instructions such as "do your arm this way or that way." The biggest challenge is to convey his style accurately and meaningfully. Some of the elements I work on are making the movements big without losing the lightness and always working with more energy—bend more; jump higher—as in Balanchine's frequent statement of the adage, "Don't save it, there is only today."

There were reasons why Mr. B did certain things in his choreography, and what he wanted is inherent in the movement. He wanted no pretense, just full-out, honest dancing. Everything is built into the choreography if it is danced that way. "Don't think. Just dance," he used to say, meaning not to overanalyze but rather for a dancer to trust her intuitive and kinesthetic responses. People who get offended by the statement may interpret it as his meaning that dancers shouldn't ever think, but the statement is about absorbing yourself in the physicality of the moment. These aspects of his choreography and teaching are best conveyed through performing his work, not just through talking about it or even taking class. That is why it is really gratifying to stage his dances here at Purchase and other places.

My work at Purchase and outside it kept me very busy, but I did also enjoy a meaningful personal life. After my divorce, I had a couple of relationships with other men, but those relationships did not work out. Then, in early 1997, my friends Bob and Joan Ellis asked me, "How would you like to meet a really nice man?" Bob had met the man in question, Howard Garson, through a self-help group. I had met the

Ellises when I lived in Armonk with my first husband, Bill. We had been neighbors and my son played with their son. I said I would love to meet a very nice man.

Months went by and no introduction was forthcoming. Finally, I was invited to the Ellises for a dinner and was told Howard would be there. What I remember most as I walked into their kitchen was Howard's spontaneous and utterly sweet smile and how his face lit up when he saw me. He seemed very nice, and we talked about our respective divorces, but I remember thinking that he was too old for me. I was fifty-four, and he was fifteen years my senior. He asked me for my phone number when I was leaving, and I gave it to him. It was not love at first sight.

Howard called a few days later and invited me to dinner. We sat across from one another, and our hands touched, and I was sort of surprised to feel a thrill—chemistry was there. So we started dating, but he never made a pass at me. I later found out that he was such a gentleman that he didn't want me to think that he was only interested in one thing.

Howard proposed to me in July of 1997. We were having dinner in Gus's restaurant in Harrison, New York. I had driven home on a Friday from teaching in Carlisle, Pennsylvania, to see him for the weekend. I kind of knew what was coming, but I started to cry with joy when he asked me. That Saturday we drove up to Connecticut to see his friend Marty Levey, who owned an estate jewelry business, to pick out an engagement ring. I was so excited. I picked out a three-stone ring with a diamond in the middle and rubies on either side. It was the most beautiful ring I had ever seen. I drove back to Carlisle wearing the ring and looking down at it while my hands were on the steering wheel. I couldn't wait to show it to all my fellow teachers in Carlisle.

Howard and I were married in November of 1997 at the National Arts Club in Gramercy Park, in New York City. It is a beautiful place, lots of stained glass, a feel of ancient splendor. We did not go on a honeymoon but went to Switzerland, in 2000, for a reunion of Howard's medical school colleagues. We considered that trip a honeymoon.

We were married for sixteen-and-a-half years, and they were some of the happiest years of my life. We never fought, and we loved each other

Howard and me, at our wedding, 1997. Photo by Helene Wainston.

very much. Howard taught me what it meant to truly love somebody, and I feel so lucky that I had those years with him. I often wished we had met sooner because we were so right for each other. He adored me and was so proud of my career on the stage. And I adored him. We lived in a townhouse in White Plains (in Westchester and close to Purchase).

Howard was a member of the Unitarian Church there. He was Jewish, but he had been drawn to the church. I joined also, although it was more his thing than mine. After Howard retired, he would accompany me everywhere when I traveled for Purchase College. We became inseparable, and I used to worry what it would be like when he was no longer around to go everywhere with me.

With Howard's support, I took on increasing responsibilities. From 2003 to 2010, I was artistic director of the Purchase College version of *The Nutcracker*, with choreography by me and other members of the faculty. It was a great moneymaker for scholarships for dance students and provided funding for our spring concerts. Most of the dance majors were involved (nearly 100), and we used around 200 children from the community. This production was always magical. Different faculty members would take on various parts of the choreography, so it was very collaborative, and the dances involved modern choreography as well as ballet. We made changes every year to adjust to new dancers and our own new ideas. When we auditioned children from the community, we looked not so much for dance technique as for something that drew one to the dancer, a performance energy. Our Claras were always performed by children rather than adults because of children's innate innocence, charm, and freshness. Our first Clara, Skylar Brandt, is a soloist today with American Ballet Theatre. Another of our Claras, Catherine Hurlin, was promoted to soloist at American Ballet Theatre in 2018. The stage is a magical place, so it was wonderful to share with all the children who performed in this production through the years.

Our Sugar Plum Fairy and her Cavalier were danced by guest artists, including Jared Angle, Ashley Bouder, Albert Evans, Judith Fugate, Lourdes Lopez, and Damian Woetzel from New York City Ballet and Julie Diana Hench and Zachary Hench from the Pennsylvania Ballet. Bouder and Angle had been my students at Central Pennsylvania Youth Ballet, so it was remarkable to come full circle from teaching them as children to seeing them become stars of New York City Ballet and then to hire them as leads for this production. *The Nutcracker* really was an enormous affair at Purchase and very time-consuming. Its preparation basically took up the whole fall semester. But it was a labor of love. The music is so beautiful. I had danced in *The Nutcracker* myself with NYCB for eleven years, but I never tired of it. I brought my love of the music and the story to each production, whether I was dancing or directing.

Around 2006, my mother and several family members, including my cousin Barbara, drove up to see the Purchase production of *The Nutcracker* that I had directed. Barbara's grandson, Sasha, was a baby mouse, and he had just turned five. My mother was in her nineties; this was one of the last times we were all together as a family. We went together to celebrate at an Italian restaurant after the performance, and we were all talking about how wonderful everything was. Suddenly, my mother said, "I don't know. I think I would have done the party scene differently." I was so tired that I had a knee-jerk response. Instead of just ignoring her, I said, "What would you have done?" She responded, "I don't know, but something different." It really was hurtful. It just seemed to be impossible for her to say, "You did a great job." As much as she was proud of me, she would always have something critical to say. She couldn't give a compliment without cutting me in some way. I am proud of my work at Purchase, and I wanted, even needed, her praise, not her criticism. But that was just who she was.

My mother passed away on January 3, 2013, at the age of 104. She was in a nursing home toward the end of her life. She didn't have any major physical issues, but her mind was beginning to go, and she had developed dementia. Her health throughout her life had been amazing. She said it was because she stayed away from doctors. She hated them and hospitals. When her father was dying in the hospital, she could not bring herself to visit, and when I was in the hospital after a hysterectomy, she was barely able to visit. But she was very strong until close to the end of her life. Later in her final years, when she lived in Manhattan and Howard and I were living in Westchester, she would come visit me, and we would go shopping at Loehmann's and TJ Maxx. Howard and I also often had dinner with her. She would come up to Westchester, and then she would not let us drive her home afterward. She would rather take two buses to get home than to worry about us driving back, the two of us, to Westchester. We always tried to convince her to let us drive her, but to no avail. She was not easy to get along with. She could be very argumentative. I confronted her about it once, when she was on in years. I said, "Why can't you just agree with me, even once?" She didn't respond, but she got a terrible case of indigestion, and then I felt guilty.

My mother was incredibly smart. She could have done some wonderful things. She would have been a great buyer in fashion or a manager of any kind. She really managed my whole life from theater to ballet to my teaching at Purchase. She was a great strategic thinker. I don't think I ever grew out of wanting and needing her validation and praise, but I have increasingly found professional validation for my work as a teacher and choreographer.

Shortly before my mother died, after having had a minor procedure on my right breast, I unfortunately developed an infection which resulted in an open wound which would not heal. This was called a fistula, and the only way to get rid of a fistula is by surgery. The surgery really deformed my breast, and I was told I should have plastic surgery. I returned to work at the college a week after the initial surgery and was in my office when Howard called and said I needed to come home right away. He wouldn't say why, but I had a feeling the news wasn't good. As soon as I got home, Howard told me that the doctor had called and that the biopsy of the tissue that had been removed from my breast during the surgery had revealed microscopic cancer cells. I called the doctor and learned that I had DCIS, ductal carcinoma in situ.

The doctor recommended a mastectomy because he did not know for sure whether there was, as he put it, "a big cancer" under the infection and that the best way to be sure would be to remove all the breast tissue. Howard and I scheduled the surgery and visited the plastic surgeon to discuss the implant which would be done at the same time. Howard helped me process the impact of this sudden and devastating turn of events. Fortunately, there was no big cancer. The cells were confined to the milk ducts, with no lump anywhere in the breast, so I did not need chemo or radiation therapy. I was very lucky. Ironically it was because the initial infection failed to heal that the cancer cells were discovered before anything worse might have happened.

Howard was my rock throughout this ordeal. He was my nurse when I needed him and helped me stay strong emotionally. He used to say that we are all fragile creatures—our bodies work well until they don't.

Despite having several cancers, Howard had an incredible attitude about life. He never let anything stop him, and he didn't mope about because he had health problems. I think his attitude sustained him and enabled him to live as long as he did. Following his example, I try to live each day as it comes and not worry too much about the future.

My darling Howard died suddenly on April 29, 2014, a week after his eighty-sixth birthday and just a year and a half after my mother passed away. On his way to his Tuesday doubles tennis game, he was walking up the path to the tennis courts at Lake Isle Country Club in Eastchester, New York, when he fell forward on his face. He never tried to break his fall, which makes me think he was dead before he hit the ground. The day was a nightmare. As I finished my breakfast, the call came, which I had always dreaded, and the voice telling me "something has happened to your husband." A friend and tennis partner was walking behind him and saw him lying on the ground and tried to administer CPR. The paramedics were called, and they called me. I kept asking if he was conscious, and they wouldn't tell me. I knew. They took him to the emergency room at Lawrence Hospital, in Bronxville. I drove down there in a fog. They ushered me into a little room, and I sat with Howard's friend Elliot, who had been kind enough to wait there for me so I wouldn't be alone. Soon a doctor came in to say he was gone. I went into the room where he was lying with a sheet over him. They had tried to intubate him, and the mask was still on his face. His hair was matted from blood when he had fallen forward, and his face was bruised. All I could say was "My poor darling." I thank God he didn't suffer, and he went quickly. I don't think I would have been able to watch him suffer, hooked up to tubes in a hospital bed. In a split second, my life, my beautiful, wonderful life, had changed. I drove myself home.

Unless one experiences such a sudden loss, one cannot really understand what it is to go through what I just described. The panic, fear, terrible sadness, despair, shock, confusion; my heart was broken. Who would take care of me? Whom could I depend on? Luckily, I had my work at the college, which kept me busy and around people. But it was the nights and weekends alone in my house that were the most difficult. I had become so dependent on his constant, loving presence, and it has

Teaching at Purchase College, 2017. Photo by Paige DeMaio.

been very difficult getting used to being without him. Even now, I still feel a sense of loneliness, but time does, in fact, heal. My work at Purchase in passing on Balanchine's legacy has helped me with this. It gives my life meaning and a kind of central purpose.

Chapter 6

Final Thoughts on the Legacy of Balanchine

So what is Balanchine's genius? How do I view his work? So much has already been written about them.

However, I did have the distinction of working with him and observing how he developed choreography. Always prepared, he would come into the studio and start working right away. He was very specific about the steps but also allowed for dancers' individual styles and ways of moving. We were "showing" the movement as he was visualizing the music. Music was paramount for Mr. B, and since I was particularly musical, I felt he really appreciated that part of my dancing. His choreography was not meant to be internal but to be shown, presented, but without fake smiles. He also knew how to make us look good. He knew us as individuals and knew our strengths (and our weaknesses) and gave or created roles based on that knowledge.

Mr. B, although Russian by birth, completely embraced the American spirit—independent, strong, athletic, exploratory, and fast. He translated these qualities into dance, while also incorporating an abstract aesthetic that was dominating other art forms in his lifetime. He focused on time, structure, and form—particularly line. He had an enormous effect on the dance world. I remember seeing the Royal Ballet, for instance, back in the 1960s, and they were so proper and placed—there was no stretching of the line. I saw them recently, and they now stretch their lines and exaggerate positions. Every company is doing this, from the more traditional, like American Ballet Theatre, to the less traditional, like Pina Bausch Tanztheater Wuppertal. That stretched line is now de rigueur. I attribute this to Balanchine. But the extent of his influence goes far beyond the stretched line.

The Oxford English Dictionary defines a genius as "a person who is

From left to right: Me, Michael Arshansky, Mr. B, Larry O'Brien, and Roger Pietrucha rehearsing *Harlequinade*, 1965. Photo by Martha Swope ©Billy Rose Theatre Division, The New York Public Library for the Performing Arts.

exceptionally intelligent or creative, either generally or in some particular respect."[1] Balanchine was, of course, exceptionally intelligent and creative, which is easily seen in his work. What resonates beyond the above definition is described in the publication *Psychology Today*, in an article titled "Can We Define Genius?" by Andrew Robinson: "Genius is the name we give to a quality of work that transcends fashion, fame, and reputation: the opposite of a period piece. Genius abolishes both the time and the place of its origin."[2] The key word is "transcends." When I think of dancing some Balanchine ballets, I find myself describing an almost religious experience—a marriage of exquisite music, visualized by exquisite choreography to produce an incredible, transcendent, physical satisfaction. I had that experience dancing ballets such as *Serenade, Concerto Barocco,* and *Allegro Brillante*. Choreographed so many years ago, his ballets abolish the time and the place of their origin. His creative mind seemed to know no bounds. His ability to produce choreography on union time was staggering. Day after day, he was in the studio working, creating ballets. Not every single one was a masterpiece, but a huge number were. To call him the greatest choreographer of the twentieth century is no understatement, even though the twentieth century was overflowing with innovations and evolutions in dance, led by an array of gifted choreographers.

I see the 1960s as being the "Golden Years" of NYCB and of Balanchine as a choreographer, and I was truly lucky to have been a part of the company and part of Mr. B's work then. Those of us who danced for him personally share something unique and special. We are a genteel community, a family. I am proud to be a part of that community as a former member of NYCB and part of the future as I share my knowledge with my students and continue Balanchine's legacy.

New York City Ballet reunion at Karin von Aroldingen's apartment, circa 1984. I am at the top of fire escape on far left and Karin is next to me. Photo by Arthur Elgort.

Acknowledgments

There are many people we the authors would like to thank. First and foremost, Bettijane Sills would like to thank her late husband, Howard S. Garson, who took such pride in her accomplishments and always encouraged her to write a memoir. She would like to thank Lucille Werlinich, without whose support this book might not have been written, as well as Dennis Mallach, who was an excellent "sounding board." Mindy Aloff, dance editor for the University Press of Florida, offered insightful and detailed comments and edits that helped shape the final form of the book. Linda Bathgate, deputy director and editor in chief for the University Press of Florida, gave much-needed support and assistance. Joel Cadman, Elizabeth McPherson's husband, scanned and processed photos. Lynne Stetson Forrest (former New York City Ballet dancer) and Barbara Ley Toffler (Sills's cousin) generously contributed their memories. Joan Ellis assisted by typing up several pages of the book in the early phases of Sills's writing. Lastly, many thanks to the New York Public Library, Paige DeMaio, Arthur Elgort, Ted Kivitt, Gabriel Pinski, Bill Rosenthal, and Helene Wainston for permission to use photographs.

Appendix A

New York City Ballet Premières
in Which Bettijane Sills Performed

Raymonda Variations (originally titled *Valses et Variations*)
Choreography by George Balanchine
Music by Alexander Glazounov
Première: December 7, 1961

A Midsummer Night's Dream
Choreography by George Balanchine
Music by Felix Mendelssohn
Première: January 17, 1962

Noah and the Flood
Choreography by George Balanchine
Music by Igor Stravinsky
Première: June 14, 1962, CBS-TV Broadcast

The Chase or The Vixen's Choice (1963)
Choreography by Jacques d'Amboise
Music by Wolfgang Amadeus Mozart
Première: September 18, 1963

Clarinade
Choreography by George Balanchine
Music by Morton Gould
Première April 29, 1964

Irish Fantasy
Choreography by Jacques d'Amboise
Music by Charles Camille Saint-Saëns
Première: August 12, 1964

Harlequinade (original "Scaramouche" couple)
Choreography by George Balanchine
Music by Riccardo Drigo
Première: February 4, 1965

Don Quixote
Choreography by George Balanchine
Music by Nicolas Nabokov
Première: May 28, 1965

Divertimento No. 15
Choreography by George Balanchine
Music by Wolfgang Amadeus Mozart
Première: April 27, 1966

Jewels [Diamonds]
Choreography by George Balanchine
Music by Gabriel Fauré, Igor Stravinsky, and Peter Ilyitch Tchaikovsky
Première: April 13, 1967

Requiem Canticles
Choreography by George Balanchine
Music by Igor Stravinsky
Première: May 2, 1968

Tschaikovsky Suite No. 3
Choreography by George Balanchine
Music by: Peter Ilyitch Tchaikovsky
Première: December 3, 1970

Who Cares?
Choreography by George Balanchine
Music by George Gershwin
Première: February 5, 1970

Goldberg Variations
Choreography by Jerome Robbins
Music by Johann Sebastian Bach
Première: May 27, 1971

Divertimento from "Le Baiser de la Fée" (a reworking of the 1937 original)
Choreography by George Balanchine
Music by Igor Stravinsky
Première: June 21, 1972

Serenade in A
Choreography by Todd Bolender
Music by Igor Stravinsky
Première: June 21, 1972

Appendix B

Bettijane Sills's Stagings of Balanchine Ballets

1983   *Serenade*—Purchase Dance Company

1983   The first three movements of *The Four Temperaments*—Purchase Dance Company

1984   *Valse Fantaisie* (1967)—Purchase Dance Company

1987   *Serenade*—Purchase Dance Company

1987   *Valse Fantaisie* (1967)—Purchase Dance Company

1988   Excerpts from *The Nutcracker*—Stamford City Ballet

1988   *Tarantella*—Purchase Dance Company

1988   "Elegy Section" from *Tschaikovsky, Suite No. 3*—Purchase Dance Company

1990   *Serenade*—Philadelphia School of the Arts

1991   *Serenade*—Purchase Dance Company

1991   "Elegy Section" from *Tschaikovsky, Suite No. 3*—Purchase Dance Company

1992   *Tarantella*—Purchase Dance Company

1993   Excerpts from *Who Cares?*—Purchase Dance Company

1995   Excerpts from *Stars and Stripes*—Repertory Dance Theatre

1995   *Who Cares?* (concert version)—Allegheny Ballet Company

1995   *Valse Fantaisie* [1967]—Allegheny Ballet Company

1995   *Valse Fantaisie* [1967]—Repertory Dance Theatre

1996   *Serenade*—Hong Kong Academy for the Performing Arts

1996   "Elegy" from *Tschaikovsky Suite No. 3*—Columbus Youth Ballet and Martha Graham II

1997   *Tarantella*—Purchase Dance Company

1998   *Steadfast Tin Soldier*—Purchase Dance Company

2000   *Scotch Symphony*—Purchase Dance Company

2001   Excerpts from *Stars and Stripes*—Purchase Dance Company

2004   *Serenade*—Purchase Dance Company

2005   *Valse Fantaisie* [1967]—New England Dance Theatre

2006   *Allegro Brillante*—Orlando Ballet in Florida

2007   *Serenade*—Taipei National University of the Arts

2008   *The Four Temperaments*—Purchase Dance Company

2010   *Serenade*—Purchase Dance Company

2013   *Valse Fantaisie* [1967]—Purchase Dance Company

2015   "The Man I Love" section from *Who Cares?*—Purchase Dance (senior project)

2016   *The Four Temperaments*—Purchase Dance Company

2017   *Concerto Barocco*—Purchase Dance Company

Appendix C

Bettijane Sills's Choreographic Works

1979	*Waltz Scherzo* for Purchase Dance Company
1982	*Slavonic Dances* for Purchase Dance Company
1993	*Simple Symphony* for Purchase Dance Company
1994	*Secrets* for Purchase Dance Company
1995	*Four Serenades* for Columbus Youth Ballet
1998	*Serenata* for Interlochen Arts Academy
1999	*Voyage dans la Lune* for Central Pennsylvania Youth Ballet
2001	*Swinging from a Star* for Central Pennsylvania Youth Ballet
2002	*Dayful of Song* for Purchase Dance Company
2009	*Masquerade* for Central Pennsylvania Youth Ballet, also performed by New Jersey Ballet and Purchase Dance Company
2014	*Tango* for Purchase dancer senior showing
2015	*The Kiss* choreographed for Purchase Dance Company

Appendix D

Video/Film of Bettijane Sills

The Nutcracker by George Balanchine, NYCB, filmed for television (CBS-TV's Playhouse 90), 1958

Ballinade by Harry Asmus, High School of Performing Arts, 1959

Reverie by Olga Tavolga, High School of Performing Arts, 1960

Noah and the Flood by Igor Stravinsky with choreography by George Balanchine, NYCB, filmed for television 1962

New York City Ballet in Montreal, Vol. 4, filmed in Canada, 1964 (B. Sills in *The Four Temperaments* by George Balanchine)

Don Quixote by George Balanchine, NYCB, 1965

Concerto Barocco by George Balanchine, 1966, https://www.youtube.com/watch?v=fwYwIOer3sc

A Midsummer Night's Dream by George Balanchine, NYCB, dir. Balanchine and Dan Eriksen, 1967

Brahms-Schoenberg Quartet by George Balanchine, 1969

Episodes by George Balanchine, 1969

Raymonda Variations by George Balanchine, 1969

Concerto Barocco by George Balanchine, 1969

La Valse by George Balanchine, 1969

Jewels: "Diamonds" by George Balanchine, 1970

Le New York City Ballet: Une école, *un style, une compagnie, un repertoire,* filmed in Canada 1971 (B. Sills in *Who Cares?* and *Movements for Piano and Orchestra,* both by Balanchine)

Gala Performance: To Save the Dance Collection (B. Sills in *The Concert* by Jerome Robbins), 1972

Interviewed for documentary *In Balanchine's Classroom,* dir. Connie Hochman, not yet released

ॐ

Films listed that are not commercially available can be viewed at The Jerome Robbins Dance Division of The New York Public Library for the Performing Arts in New York City.

Appendix E

Bettijane Sills's Roles in Broadway Productions

One of the three children (replaced one of the original children) in *The Wisteria Trees*, Martin Beck Theatre, March 29, 1950–September 16, 1950

Jane Baxter in *Seventeen*, Broadhurst Theatre, June 21, 1951–November 24, 1951

One of the three children in *Seventh Heaven*, ANTA Playhouse, May 26, 1955–July 2, 1955

Notes

Chapter 1. Child Actor

1. "Music Hall Gets Smallens," *Billboard*, July 12, 1947: 42. No author.

2. "Smallens Shakes Music Hall Ork.," *Billboard*, September 13, 1947: 44. No author.

3. Ibid.

4. Ibid.

5. Sherry Bowen, "Children Seen on TV Work Long, Hard Years," *Democrat and Chronicle*, September 28, 1952: 3C.

6. Carolyn Crowley, "Meet Me at the Automat," *Smithsonian Magazine*, August 2001. Accessed September 12, 2017. http://www.smithsonianmag.com/arts-culture/meet-me-at-the-automat-47804151/.

7. "Plays out of Town," *Variety*, May 29, 1951: 58. No author.

8. Brooks Atkinson, "At the Theatre," *New York Times*, June 22, 1951: 16L.

9. Arthur Pollock, "'Seventeen' Brings Back Charm of Tarkington's 1907 Indiana," *Daily Compass*, June 22, 1951.

10. John Chapman, "Nice Young People, but Few Songs in Musical Version of Seventeen," *Daily News*, June 22, 1951: 55.

11. Walter Winchell, "Of New York," *New York Daily Mirror*, June 24, 1951: 10.

12. Marie Torre, "'Seventeen' a Light Innocent Musical," *New York World-Telegram and Sun*, June 22, 1951: 12.

13. Lewis Funke, "Theatre: 'Seventh Heaven' Set to Music," *New York Times*, May 27, 1955: 16L.

14. Charles Witbeck, "Joey Couldn't Be All Bad," *Ashbury Park Press*, April 17, 1964: 22.

15. Hedda Hopper, "In Hollywood: Churchill's Memoirs Rolling in England," *Detroit Free Press*, July 25, 1960: 18.

Chapter 2. Becoming a Dancer

1. Iris Rifkin-Gainer and Blanche Evan, "An Interview with Blanche Evan," *American Journal of Dance Therapy* 5.1 (December 1982): 5.

2. "Obituaries—Harry Asmus," *Dance Magazine* (June 1977): 17–18.

3. Jennifer Dunning, *But First a School* (New York: Viking Penguin, 1985), photo insert after p. 84.

4. Ibid, p. 101.

Chapter 3. New York City Ballet, Corps de Ballet

1. "New York City Ballet 1960–69," New York City Ballet website. Accessed January 20, 2017. https://www.nycballet.com/Explore/Our-History/NYCB-Chronology/1960-1969. aspx.

2. Leonard Lyons, "The Lyons Den," *New York Post*, February 24, 1970: 39.

3. Nancy Lassalle and Suki Schorer, *Balanchine Teaching* (New York: Eakins Press, 2016), 3.

4. "Advertisement," *Kingston Daily Freeman*, July 2, 1961: 8.

5. "New York City Ballet 1960–69," New York City Ballet website. Accessed January 20, 2017. https://www.nycballet.com/Explore/Our-History/NYCB-Chronology/1960-1969. aspx.

6. "History," Ravinia web site. Accessed January 31, 2018. https://www.ravinia.org/Page/ History.

7. "Marnee Morris (1946–2011)," *Dance Magazine*, September 19, 2011. Accessed February 14, 2011. http://www.dancemagazine.com/marnee-morris-1946aeur-2011-2306885436. html.

8. Ibid.

9. Ibid.

10. Robert Gottlieb, ed., *Reading Dance: A Gathering of Memoirs, Reportage, Criticism, Profiles, Interviews, and Some Uncategorizable Extras* (New York: Pantheon, 2008), 195–96.

11. Clement Crisp, "New York City Ballet," *Financial Times*, Sept. 7, 1965: 22.

12. John Martin, "Ballet: 8 Stars in 'Agon,'" *New York Times*, May 3, 1962: L26.

13. Walter Terry, "The City Has a Royal Ballet in Dream," *I Was There: Selected Dance Reviews and Articles—1936–1976* (New York: Marcel Dekker, 1978), 413–14.

14. Walter Terry, "June 15, 1962: Noah and the Flood," *I Was There: Selected Dance Reviews and Articles—1936–1976* (New York: Marcel Dekker, 1978), 417–18.

15. Rachel Marcy, "Dancers and Diplomats: New York City Ballet in Moscow, October 1962," *The Appendix: Futures of the Past*, September 9, 2014. Accessed February 1, 2016. http://theappendix.net/issues/2014/7/dancers-and-diplomats-new-york-city-ballet-in-moscow-october-1962.

16. Clare Croft, "Ballet Nations: The New York City Ballet's 1962 US State Department-Sponsored Tour of the Soviet Union," *Theatre Journal* 61.3 (2009): 427. Accessed February 1, 2016.

http://amdreamcomp.pbworks.com/w/file/fetch/93496388/61.3.croft.pdf.

17. Ibid.

18. Ibid.

19. Rachel Marcy, n.p.

20. "New York City Ballet Hailed by Newspapers of Vienna," *New York Times*, October 2, 1962: L47.

21. Ibid.

22. Rachel Marcy, n.p.

23. John Martin, "Ballet: Visit to Bolshoi," *New York Times*, October 10, 1962: L59.

24. Ibid.

25. Ibid.

26. Clare Croft, n.p.

27. John Martin, "New York City Ballet Is Success in Soviet Union," *New York Times*, October 22, 1962: L34.

28. John Martin, "City Ballet Ends Leningrad Stand," *New York Times*, November 9, 1962: 32L.

29. Joel Lobenthal, *Alla Osipenko: Beauty and Resistance in Soviet Ballet* (New York: Oxford University Press, 2016), 116.

30. Rachel Marcy, n.p.

31. John Martin, "Ballet: Visit to Bolshoi," *New York Times*, October 10, 1962: L59.

32. Elizabeth Souritz, "Balanchine in Russia," *Ballet Review* (Spring 2011): 55. Accessed February 1, 2016. http://www.balletreview.com/images/Ballet_Review_39-1_Balanchine_in_Russia.pdf.

33. Rachel Marcy, n.p.

34. Richard Buckle, *George Balanchine: Ballet Master* (London: Penguin Books, 1988): 236.

Chapter 4. New York City Ballet, Soloist

1. Lynn Garafola, ed., with Eric Foner, *Dance for a City: Fifty Years of the New York City Ballet* (New York: Columbia University Press, 1999), 18.

2. Douglas Turnbaugh, "Good Guys vs. Bad Guys at Lincoln Center," *New York Magazine*, May 20, 1968: 51.

3. Garafola, 25.

4. Ibid.

5. Nancy Reynolds, *Repertory in Review: 40 Years of the New York City Ballet* (New York: Dial Press, 1977), 227.

6. Allen Hughes, "Two 'New' Ballets—'Dim Lustre' and 'Clarinade,'" *New York Times*, May 24, 1964: X22.

7. Ibid.

8. Lynne Stetson, interview with Elizabeth McPherson and Bettijane Sills, July 29, 2015.

9. Ibid.

10. Ibid.

11. Ibid.

12. Reynolds, 232.

13. Walter Terry, "*Harlequinade*—A Hit," *I Was There: Selected Dance Reviews and Articles—1936–1976* (New York: Marcel Dekker, 1978), 473.

14. Edwin Denby, *Dance Writings* (New York: Alfred A. Knopf, 1986), 485.

15. Clive Barnes, "Dance: 'Divertimento': Balanchine and Mozart Excel at State Theater, but Designer Does Them Wrong," *New York Times*, April 28, 1966: L51.

16. Clive Barnes, "Ballet: Our Revels Now Are Ended at the Old Metropolitan," *New York Times*, May 9, 1966: L48.

17. "New York City Ballet Here in July with Jewels," *Montreal Gazette*, June 13, 1967: 23, no author. Accessed September 11, 2017. https://news.google.com/newspapers?nid=1946&dat=19670613&id=oZ4tAAAAIBAJ&sjid=BqAFAAAAIBAJ&pg=6025,2699132&hl=en.

18. Robert Garis, "The New York City Ballet," *Partisan Review* (Fall 1968): 581. Accessed September 9, 2017. *http://www.bu.edu/partisanreview/books/PR1968V35N4/HTML/files/assets/basic-html/index.html*.

19. "New York City Ballet Here in July with Jewels," *Montreal Gazette*, June 13, 1967: 23, no author. Accessed September 11, 2017.
https://news.google.com/newspapers?nid=1946&dat=19670613&id=oZ4tAAAAIBAJ&sjid=BqAFAAAAIBAJ&pg=6025,2699132&hl=en.

20. Clive Barnes, "Dance: City Ballet Takes Edinburgh," *New York Times*, August 31, 1967: L28.

21. Clive Barnes, "Dance: The Balanchine of '36 and '68." *New York Times*, May 4, 1968: L45.

22. Suzanne Farrell, *Holding On to the Air: An Autobiography* (Gainesville: University Press of Florida, 2002), 182–83.

23. Ibid., 187.

24. Anna Kisselgoff, "Dance: It's 'The Nutcracker' Season," *New York Times*, December 6, 1968: L53.

25. Marcia B. Siegel, "Another Opening," *At the Vanishing Point: A Critic Looks at Dance* (New York: Saturday Review Press, 1972), 29–30.

26. Clive Barnes, "Dance: Duo-Tchaikovsky." *New York Times*, December 4, 1970: L55.

27. Clive Barnes, "Dance: Balanchine Offers 'PAMTGG,'" *New York Times*, June 18, 1971: L27.

28. Siegel, 27.

29. Clive Barnes, "Dance: A Rare 'Concert': City Ballet Gives New Version of '56 Work," *New York Times*, December 4, 1971: L23.

30. Walter Terry, "Dance Laughter," *I Was There: Selected Dance Reviews and Articles—1936–1976* (New York: Marcel Dekker, 1978), 600.

31. Joseph H. Mazo. "The Dance," *Women's Wear Daily*, December 6, 1971: 12.

32. Jack Anderson, "New York Newsletter," *Dancing Times* (February 1972): 244.

33. Clive Barnes, "Dance: A Particularly Festive Mood," *New York Times*, May 20, 1972: L21.

34. Walter Terry, "The Genius of Robbins," *I Was There: Selected Dance Reviews and Articles—1936–1976* (New York: Marcel Dekker, 1978), 590.

35. "New York City Ballet 1970–79." www.nycballet.com. Accessed February 3, 2018. https://www.nycballet.com/Explore/Our-History/NYCB-Chronology/1960-1969.aspx.

36. Arlene Croce, "Dancing: Blind Fate," *New Yorker* (December 2, 1974): 150.

37. Reynolds, 294.

Chapter 5. Teacher, Répétiteur, and Choreographer

1. Allegra Kent, *Once a Dancer . . . An Autobiography* (Gainesville: University Press of Florida, 1997), 250–51.

2. "Purchase College History," Purchase College website. Accessed September 12, 2017. https://www.purchase.edu/AboutPurchase/History.aspx.

3. Gia Kourlas, "Barbara Weisberger, a Former Balanchine Protégée, Still Champions

Ballet," *New York Times*, September 3, 2006: AR6. Accessed January 31, 2018. http://www.nytimes.com/2006/09/03/arts/dance/03kour.html.

4. Ibid.

5. Jennifer Dunning, "Review/Dance; The Dancers at Purchase, In an Annual Spring Rite," *New York Times*, March 1, 1993: C10L.

6. Robert Johnson, "'Masquerade' Review: New Work Livens New Jersey Ballet's Spooky Fall Lineup," *Star-Ledger*, November 23, 2010.

7. Ibid.

8. Nancy Turano, discussion with Elizabeth McPherson, June 15, 2017.

9. Jennifer Dunning, "Dance in Review: Purchase Dance Corps," *New York Times*, April 15, 1991: C12L. http://www.nytimes.com/1991/04/15/arts/dance-in-review-624291.html.

10. Anna Kisselgoff, "Critic's Notebook; Balanchine's '34 Ballet, Staged at Its Original Spot," *New York Times*, April 20, 2004: E3.

11. Mindy Aloff, "Letter from New York," *DanceView Times*, New York Edition, April 19, 2004. Accessed July 10, 2016. http://danceviewtimes.com/dvny/aloff/spring04/041904.htm.

Chapter 6. Final Thoughts on the Legacy of Balanchine

1. "Genius," Oxford Dictionaries. Accessed July 10, 2016. http://www.oxforddictionaries.com/us/definition/american_english/genius.

2. Andrew Robinson, "Can We Define Genius?" *Psychology Today* (November 30, 2010). Accessed July 10, 2016. https://www.psychologytoday.com/blog/sudden genius/201011/can-we-define-genius.

Bibliography

Advertisement. *Kingston Daily Freeman*, July 2, 1961: 8.

Aloff, Mindy. "Letter from New York." *DanceView Times*. New York Edition. April 19, 2004. Accessed July 10, 2016. http://danceviewtimes.com/dvny/aloff/spring04/041904.htm.

Anderson, Jack. "New York Newsletter." *Dancing Times*, February 1972: 244.

Atkinson, Brooks. "At the Theatre." *New York Times*, June 22, 1951: 16L.

Barnes, Clive. "Ballet: Our Revels Now Are Ended at the Old Metropolitan." *New York Times*, May 9, 1966: L48.

———. "Dance: A Particularly Festive Mood." *New York Times*, May 20, 1972: L21.

———. "Dance: A Rare 'Concert': City Ballet Gives New Version of '56 Work." *New York Times*, December 4, 1971: L23.

———. "Dance: Balanchine Offers 'PAMTGG.'" *New York Times*, June 18, 1971: L27.

———. "Dance: City Ballet Takes Edinburgh." *New York Times*, August 31, 1967: L28.

———. "Dance: 'Divertimento': Balanchine and Mozart Excel at State Theater, but Designer Does Them Wrong." *New York Times*, April 28, 1966: L51.

———. "Dance: Duo-Tchaikovsky." *New York Times*, December 4, 1970: L55.

———. "Dance: The Balanchine of '36 and '68." *New York Times*, May 4, 1968: L45.

Bowen, Sherry. "Children Seen on TV Work Long, Hard Years." *Democrat and Chronicle*, September 28, 1952: 3C.

Buckle, Richard. *George Balanchine: Ballet Master*. London: Penguin Books, 1988.

Chapman, John. "Nice Young People but Few Songs in Musical Version of Seventeen." *Daily News*, June 22, 1951: 55.

Crisp, Clement. "New York City Ballet." *Financial Times*, September 7, 1965: 22.

Croce, Arlene. "Dancing: Blind Fate." *New Yorker*, December 2, 1974: 146–51.

Croft, Clare. "Ballet Nations: The New York City Ballet's 1962 US State Department–Sponsored Tour of the Soviet Union." *Theatre Journal* 61.3 (2009): 421–42. Accessed February 1, 2016. http://amdreamcomp.pbworks.com/w/file/fetch/93496388/61.3.croft.pdf.

Crowley, Carolyn Hughes. "Meet Me at the Automat." *Smithsonian Magazine*, August 2001. Accessed September 12, 2017. https://www.smithsonianmag.com/arts-culture/meet-me-at-the-automat-47804151/.

Denby, Edwin. *Dance Writings*. New York: Alfred A. Knopf, 1986.

Dunning, Jennifer. *But First a School*. New York: Viking Penguin, 1985.

———. "Dance in Review: Purchase Dance Corps." *New York Times*, April 15, 1991: C12L.

Accessed September 12, 2017. http://www.nytimes.com/1991/04/15/arts/dance-in-re-view-624291.html.

———. "Review/Dance; The Dancers at Purchase, In an Annual Spring Rite." *New York Times*, March 1, 1993: C10L.

Farrell, Suzanne. *Holding on to the Air: An Autobiography*. Gainesville: University Press of Florida, 2002.

Funke, Lewis. "Theatre: 'Seventh Heaven' Set to Music." *New York Times*, May 27, 1955: 16L.

Garafola, Lynn, ed., with Eric Foner. *Dance for a City: Fifty Years of the New York City Ballet*. New York: Columbia University Press, 1999.

Garis, Robert. "The New York City Ballet," *Partisan Review*, Fall 1968: 573–83. Accessed September 9, 2017. http://www.bu.edu/partisanreview/books/PR1968V35N4/HTML/files/assets/basic-html/index.htmlNo. 581.

"Genius." Oxford Dictionaries. Accessed July 10, 2016. http://www.oxforddictionaries.com/us/definition/american_english/genius.

Gottlieb, Robert, ed. *Reading Dance: A Gathering of Memoirs, Reportage, Criticism, Profiles, Interviews, and Some Uncategorizable Extras*. New York: Pantheon, 2008.

"History." Ravinia website. Accessed January 31, 2018. https://www.ravinia.org/Page/History.

Hopper, Hedda. "In Hollywood: Churchill's Memoirs Rolling in England." *Detroit Free Press*, July 25, 1960: 18.

Hughes, Allen. "Two 'New' Ballets—'Dim Lustre' and 'Clarinade.'" *New York Times*, May 24, 1964: X22.

Johnson, Robert. "'Masquerade' Review: New Work Livens New Jersey Ballet's Spooky Fall Lineup." *Star-Ledger*, November 23, 2010.

Kent, Allegra. *Once a Dancer . . . An Autobiography*. Gainesville: University Press of Florida, 1997.

Kisselgoff, Anna. "Dance: It's 'The Nutcracker' Season." *New York Times,* December 6, 1968: L53.

———. "Critic's Notebook; Balanchine's '34 Ballet, Staged at Its Original Spot. *New York Times*, April 20, 2004: E3.

Kourlas, Gia. "Barbara Weisberger, a Former Balanchine Protégée, Still Champions Ballet." *New York Times*, September 3, 2006: AR6. Accessed January 31, 2018. http://www.nytimes.com/2006/09/03/arts/dance/03kour.html.

Lassalle, Nancy, and Suki Schorer. *Balanchine Teaching*. New York: Eakins Press, 2016.

Lobenthal, Joel. *Alla Osipenko: Beauty and Resistance in Soviet Ballet*. New York: Oxford University Press, 2016.

Lyons, Leonard. "The Lyons Den." *New York Post*, February 24, 1970: 39.

Marcy, Rachel. "Dancers and Diplomats: New York City Ballet in Moscow, October 1962." *The Appendix: Futures of the Past*, September 9, 2014. Accessed September 14, 2017. http://theappendix.net/issues/2014/7/dancers-and-diplomats-new-york-city-ballet-in-moscow-october-1962.

"Marnee Morris (1946–2011)." *Dance Magazine*, September 19, 2011. Accessed February 14, 2018. https://www.dancemagazine.com/marnee-morris-1946aeur-2011-2306885436.html.

Martin, John. "Ballet: Visit to Bolshoi." *New York Times*, October 10, 1962: L59.

———. "Ballet: 8 Stars in 'Agon.'" *New York Times*, May 3, 1962: L26.

———. "City Ballet Ends Leningrad Stand." *New York Times*, November 9, 1962: 32L.

———. "New York City Ballet Is Success in Soviet Union." *New York Times*, October 22, 1962: L34.

Mazo, Joseph H. "The Dance." *Women's Wear Daily*, December 6, 1971: 12.

"Music Hall Gets Smallens." *Billboard*, July 12, 1947: 42.

"New York City Ballet Hailed by Newspapers of Vienna." *New York Times*, October 2, 1962: L47.

"New York City Ballet Here in July with Jewels." *Montreal Gazette*, June 13, 1967: 23. Accessed September 11, 2017. https://news.google.com/newspapers?nid=1946&dat=1967 0613&id=oZ4tAAAAIBAJ&sjid=BqAFAAAAIBAJ&pg=6025,2699132&hl=en.

New York City Ballet website. New York City Ballet Chronology. https://www.nycballet.com/Explore/Our-History/NYCB-Chronology.aspx.

New York City Ballet website. Our History and Repertory. http://www.nycballet.com/explore/default.aspx.

"Obituaries—Harry Asmus." *Dance Magazine*, June 1977: 17–18.

"Plays out of Town." *Variety*, May 29, 1951: 58.

Pollock, Arthur. "'Seventeen' Brings Back Charm of Tarkington's 1907 Indiana." *Daily Compass*, June 22, 1951, early edition.

"Purchase College History." Purchase College website. Accessed September 12, 2017. https://www.purchase.edu/AboutPurchase/History.aspx.

Reynolds, Nancy. *Repertory in Review: 40 Years of the New York City Ballet*. New York: Dial Press, 1977.

Rifkin-Gainer, Iris, and Blanche Evan. "An Interview with Blanche Evan." *American Journal of Dance Therapy* 5.1 (December 1982): 5–17.

Robinson, Andrew. "Can We Define Genius?" *Psychology Today*, November 30, 2010. Accessed July 10, 2016. https://www.psychologytoday.com/blog/sudden-genius/201011/can-we-define-genius.

Siegel, Marcia B. *At the Vanishing Point: A Critic Looks at Dance*. New York: Saturday Review Press, 1972.

"Smallens Shakes Music Hall Ork." *Billboard*, September 13, 1947: 44.

Souritz, Elizabeth. "Balanchine in Russia." *Ballet Review*, Spring 2011: 48–55.

Stetson, Lynne. Interview with Elizabeth McPherson and Bettijane Sills, July 29, 2015.

Terry, Walter. *I Was There: Selected Dance Reviews and Articles—1936–1976*. New York: Marcel Dekker, 1978.

Torre, Marie. "'Seventeen' a Light Innocent Musical." *New York World-Telegram and Sun*, June 22, 1951: 12.

Turano, Nancy. Discussion with Elizabeth McPherson, June 15, 2017.

Turnbaugh, Douglas. "Good Guys vs. Bad Guys at Lincoln Center." *New York Magazine*, May 20, 1968: 51.

Winchell, Walter. "Of New York." *New York Daily Mirror*, June 24, 1951: 10.

Witbeck, Charles. "Joey Couldn't Be All Bad." *Ashbury Park Press*, April 17, 1964: 22.

Index

Page numbers in *italics* refer to photographs.

BETTIJANE SILLS, a tenured professor, has served as faculty in the Conservatory of Dance at Purchase College since 1979. She teaches ballet, stages Balanchine repertory, and choreographs for the Purchase dancers and other companies. After working as a child actor on Broadway and television, she was invited by George Balanchine to join New York City Ballet in 1961. She was promoted to soloist in 1964, dancing many solo and demi-solo roles plus principal roles in Balanchine's *Western Symphony*, *Divertimento No. 15*, and *The Nutcracker*. She received critical acclaim as "the Wife" in Jerome Robbins's 1972 revival of *The Concert*.

❧

ELIZABETH MCPHERSON is a tenured associate professor at Montclair State University and coordinator of the BA and MFA in Dance. Executive editor for the journal *Dance Education in Practice*, she is also the editor of *The Bennington School of the Dance: A History in Writings and Interviews* and author of *The Contributions of Martha Hill to American Dance and Dance Education*. She received her BFA from Juilliard, MA from the City College of New York, and PhD from New York University.